POPPY

THE DOGS TRUST DOG

Text copyright © 2009 Dogs Trust

First published in Great Britain in 2009 by Hodder Children's Books

The right of Sophia Fergus to be identified as the Author of the Work has been
asserted by her in accordance with the Copyright, Designs and Patents Act 1988.

8

A Catalogue record for this book is available from the British Library

ISBN: 978 0 340 99776 5

Book design by Janette Revill

Printed and bound in Great Britain by
CPI Bookmarque Ltd, Croydon, Surrey

The paper and board used in this paperback by Hodder Children's Books
are natural recyclable products made from wood grown in
sustainable forests. The manufacturing processes conform to the
environmental regulations of the country of origin.

Hodder Children's Books
a division of Hachette Children's Books
338 Euston Road
London NW1 3BH
An Hachette UK company
www.hachette.co.uk

DogsTrust

POPPY

THE DOGS TRUST DOG

SOPHIA FERGUS

Hodder
Children's
Books

A division of Hachette Children's Books

To Keith

Publisher's acknowledgement
With thanks to Nicole Dryburgh who
introduced us to Dogs Trust

Contents

FOREWORD
BY CLARISSA BALDWIN,
CHIEF EXECUTIVE OF DOGS TRUST

Hello,

I am the head of the largest dog welfare charity in the UK – Dogs Trust. I love my job, and am so proud of all the work this amazing charity does. When you read this book, you'll see why.

Even though I'm supposed to be the boss, for some time now I have been living in the shadow of another member of staff here at the office. She is somebody who lights up the room. She is everyone's best friend. She is both funny and charming, and nobody can resist smiling when they see her. She is Poppy the Dogs Trust's gorgeous office dog.

But Poppy is so lovely I don't mind if many of my visitors walk straight past me to shake her paw first. And I don't even mind losing the odd sandwich from my office (though a whole platter is going a bit too far).

Actually, working with Poppy is one of the best things about my job, and I know everyone else here at HQ feels the same way. We think all offices should have a dog. They make you happy. They make you laugh. They make the good times better and the not-so-good times, well, better.

Poppy has shot to fame since she has

worked with us, so the attention she receives from this book will be like water off a dog's back. If you would like to know more about what Poppy and all her friends at Dogs Trust have been up to, do visit our website at:

www.dogstrust.org.uk

Thanks for reading this book and for loving dogs as much as we do.

Bye for now,

Clarissa

An Introduction from Poppy, the Dogs Trust Dog

'Look, Poppy! Chicken!' the photographer calls out. When I hear that magic word, I lift my ears and give the camera my best doggy pose. Photographers really like the ear-lift – they think it makes me look alert, thoughtful and wise. But little do they know, much of my best thinking is done lying on my side with my legs stretched out, my eyes closed, and my ears actually not doing very much at all.

Before we begin, perhaps I should introduce myself ...

Hello, my name is Poppy. I am five-and-a-half years old, I am a lurcher, and I am a dog with a job. That's not very unusual, you may think. After all, thousands of dogs get up every morning and go to work. Guide dogs, police dogs, sheepdogs, sniffer dogs – the list of canine careers goes on and on. But nobody has a job quite like mine.

I work at the headquarters of the UK's biggest dog welfare charity, Dogs Trust, in London, and my job is to campaign for the health and happiness of dogs everywhere. Most people who work at Dogs Trust are in fact *people*, which I agree is a bit odd, so they come to me when they want a real dog's opinion on things.

I've been on more walks and in more fund-raising events for Dogs Trust than I can count. My owner Vicki is a training and behaviour adviser at the charity, so I also regularly visit its seventeen rehoming centres across the country. Can you believe the staff at those centres look after over 16,000 stray and abandoned dogs every single year? My mind still boggles when I think about that.

When I'm not out and about on visits, I spend my days at HQ, keeping my workmates company, snuffling around their wastepaper baskets and generally mulling over the doggy issues of the day. I suppose I think mostly about two things when I'm working: how we can improve life for those dogs who are less lucky than me, and chicken. In that order, I hasten to add.

I also get lots of letters and emails from the public, and it was while I was replying to one of these emails that the idea came to me. *People are so interested in me and my story*, I thought, *just think of all those other Dogs Trust dogs with remarkable tales to tell. There are so many we could write a book!*

One year later, and here it is. I hope this book helps to show how wonderful dogs are, and how hard we at Dogs Trust work to give every dog the happy life he or she deserves.

We have all sorts of fantastic doggy tales in store for you. There are stories about wonky dogs, like dear Hubble, who newspapers called the 'Ugliest Dog in Britain', and Weasel, who was born without any ears. And when you read little Jess's tale gasps and giggles are guaranteed.

There are stories about dogs who have turned their

lives around, like Arrow, and ones like Cracker and Morris who were destined to have very important careers.

You're going to meet some personal pals of mine, Megan and Mr Magoo, who also work at Dogs Trust but do very different jobs. And the story about Oakfield Old Dogs Home is certain to make you smile.

I hope you enjoy reading the stories of all these real-life outstanding hounds as much as I have enjoyed knowing them.

Remember, just by buying this book, you too are helping to support all of those dogs that Dogs Trust takes care of seven days a week, 365 days a year. Imagine those 16,000 tails wagging a thank you, just for you.

Now, if you'll excuse me, I must leave you to get on with my photoshoot ... Did someone say chicken?

With lots of love and licks,

Poppy xxx
poppy@dogstrust.org.uk

Poppy's Story

The people who work at number 17, Wakley Street, London, are always eager to get to work. Especially on a Monday morning, while most people are grumbling at their alarm clocks and burying their heads under their pillows, these lucky few folk are springing out of bed, and getting excited about the day that lies ahead at Dogs Trust HQ.

Some Dogs Trust staff travel for two hours to get to work, others live so close they can walk there, but by 9:30 a.m., the little kitchen at 17 Wakley Street is bustling with people. Everyone is busy making cups of tea for each other, pouring big bowls of cereal, filling the room with the delicious smell of toast and people are all chattering at once about the latest doggy news.

What makes these Monday mornings so particularly special, however, is that Monday is the day when Poppy the Office Dog is sure to come into work. Everybody who enters the lively little kitchen casts a glance at the shelf where Poppy's bowl is kept. If the big silver dish is missing, they smile to themselves, knowing that it is sitting on the floor upstairs, full of water, and with Poppy's furry grey muzzle buried in it.

'I'm so proud to be Poppy's owner,' says Vicki. 'Everybody just adores her, and on the days when she comes to the office I have so many visitors. As well as being lovely company at my desk, she makes me feel like a star.'

Poppy most certainly is a 'people pooch'. Everybody who says *hello* to her in the morning receives a big wag of her tail and a friendly lick.

Poppy's Story

Sometimes she stands and leans her slender body against her workmates' legs, looking up to ask them to ruffle her soft, silver fur. Other times she will roll on to her back at their feet, which is the request for them to tickle the pale pink skin on her belly.

'Poppy is so dainty she could be made of cobwebs and paper!' her colleague Krystyna likes to say as she watches Poppy trot along the walkway in front of her desk, the long strands of fur on the tips of the dog's ears gently floating up and down as she walks.

It is difficult to believe that this tall, elegant dog was once so tiny she could fit her whole furry body and long, spindly legs into a single shoe. But that was how big Poppy was when Vicki first set eyes on her.

'Before I got Poppy I had been thinking about getting a new puppy for a while,' says Vicki. 'My oldest dog had sadly passed away, and even though we still had lots of animals – three dogs and six cats – our house seemed like it was missing another doggy face.'

She knew she wanted another rescue dog, but Vicki thought for a long time about what sort of dog he or she should be. Vicki's job as a training and behaviour adviser at Dogs Trust meant she already knew lots about different breeds and crossbreeds, but thinking about all the wonderful dogs she could choose from did not make her decision any easier.

Eventually Vicki decided that she would like a lurcher. 'A lurcher is one of the sighthounds crossed with any other breed,' she explains. 'Sighthounds are dogs that have amazing eyesight and can run really fast. They can be greyhounds, whippets, salukis, Irish wolf-hounds, or deer-hounds, and if you cross one of them with any other breed you get a lurcher.

'I have always loved the type of lurcher that is a whippet crossed with a Bedlington terrier,' she goes on to say with a smile. 'Every single one I have met has been calm, easy to train and lots of fun as well. So I asked my friend Wendy at work to find out if we had any of these sorts of lurchers in our rehoming centres that needed a home, and it

turned out that we did. We had a litter of newborn puppies in Merseyside. I was over the moon.'

Richard, who was the manager of Dogs Trust Merseyside, was good friends with Vicki, and knew that she was a fantastic dog owner. Once he had even met Vicki's border collie, Meg, when Vicki had brought her to the Merseyside Centre on a training day. Meg was a lovely, happy dog, with lots of thick black and white fur and a tongue the colour of bright pink candyfloss. She was cheerful and friendly and obviously very well-loved.

So Richard was delighted that Vicki was interested in the adorable new litter of tiny lurcher pups. He sent her lots of photos of them playing together, eager for her to love them as much as he did.

'I looked at Richard's photos and there she was,' says Vicki. 'I fell in love with Poppy's beautiful grey fluff straight away. Richard had told me how sweet she was, and once I saw the pictures I just couldn't resist. I knew my search was over.'

Vicki told Richard that she wanted to meet Poppy, and he was overjoyed. After all, he had seen Poppy's mum give birth to her babies, and although he loved every dog in his care at Dogs Trust Merseyside, those little puppies had a special place in his heart.

'Sometimes people have to give up their dogs when they really don't want to,' says Richard, 'and that's what happened with Poppy's mum. Her owners had to move house and they no longer had enough space to keep her, let alone a litter of new pups. They were so upset to give her away, but they thought giving her to Dogs Trust would be the kindest thing to do. Of course we took really good care of her, and made sure her puppies were delivered safely.

'Even though it's sad seeing litters of puppies born at Dogs Trust when they don't have a proper home, seeing those tiny newborn faces is still one of my favourite parts of the job. And at Dogs Trust we do everything we can to make sure they go to live in happy, loving families, where we know they will be well-looked after.'

When Poppy was old enough to leave her mum, and had been given all her proper injections, Richard agreed to drive the pup to Dogs Trust Evesham, where Vicki met her for the first time. 'I already knew I was definitely going to take Poppy home,' Vicki remembers, 'but when I finally met her, she was even more adorable than I imagined. And when we got home and I introduced her to my other dogs and cats, they loved her just as much as I did.'

Meg the border collie took Poppy under her wing straight away. 'Meg became like a mother to Poppy, and actually she still is,' says Vicki. 'Poppy also immediately loved my Siamese cat Dylan and insisted that he play with her. I think the games were mainly Poppy's idea to be honest. Most of them seemed to involve her leaping on Dylan and chewing his neck, while Dylan just lay there and waited for her to stop. Poor Dylan understood that Poppy was just a baby though and was very patient with her.'

Only a couple of weeks after the excitement of Poppy's arrival, when everyone had started to settle into normal family life, something terrible happened.

Twelve-week-old Poppy became seriously ill and was rushed straight to the vet's. 'It was awful,' shudders Vicki. 'She had a very nasty problem with her stomach and had to stay at the vet's for two whole weeks. He had to put her on a drip to give her energy because she couldn't eat anything. It was so serious we didn't know if she would be OK or if we would lose her. She was still so tiny, it was very upsetting and scary seeing her so ill.'

Thankfully, it turned out that young Poppy was made of strong stuff. She began to recover from the sickness, and the bouncy, happy-go-lucky puppy started to shine through again. When she was eventually well enough to come home, all the people, dogs and cats in the house were so relieved that they made an even bigger fuss of her. Even Dylan the Siamese was happy to have her chewing his neck again!

Poppy eagerly lapped up all the special attention, and gave just as much love back in return. It had only been just over a month since she joined the family, but with all the worry everyone had experienced together, it was as if the little lurcher had lived with them for ever.

Meg and Poppy became inseparable. The older dog loved the youngster so dearly, and watched over her so carefully, that she even started picking up some of her lurcher habits! In a game called 'mouse jumping', little Poppy would throw a toy or a treat up in the air and then pounce on it, pretending she was a real hunter. Vicki couldn't believe it when Meg started playing the same game. 'Usually mouse jumping is a game that only lurchers play,' she laughs. 'It was so funny watching Meg playing it too.'

When Vicki watched little Poppy sleeping she felt sure that, now she had recovered from her horrible illness, the pup no longer had a care in the world. Vicki says, 'I knew Poppy was having lovely dreams because she would wag her tail while she was asleep. She still does it to this day – it's so sweet! Poppy has really noisy dreams – she growls and chortles and moves her legs like she's playing a wonderful chasing game with a rabbit.

'She makes funny noises when she's playing with her toys as well. She sort of whistles, growls and hums all at once when she's playing with her rubber pig or her rubber chicken. Poppy's funny noises are a sign of her really enjoying herself.'

It seemed to Vicki that one day Poppy was a fuzzy, shoe-sized pup, and the next she was a big, strong and graceful dog. All of a sudden, she had long, slender legs that could carry her at amazing speeds over the fields where they lived. The tiny little pegs she chewed her rubber chicken with had turned into beautiful, strong, white teeth. And what had been a tiny pink tongue now gave her owner's hand a bigger lick than ever.

It was while Vicki was accepting one of these big licks and looking down at her lovely fully-grown dog, that an idea came to her. Instead of spending the day with Vicki's mum like the three other dogs did during the week, Poppy should come to the office with her. She would be perfect to work at Dogs Trust. She was friendly and would certainly enjoy lots of dog-lovers cooing over her at once, but she was relaxed enough to not get too excited. Vicki was certain she would love Wendy's dog Reuben, who she would be sitting next to, as well as all the other dogs who came into work.

That day, Vicki asked her manager if it would be OK for Poppy to come to the office to meet everyone. He considered it for a moment and then said it would be fine. As a dog-lover himself, he was secretly very pleased.

So that was settled. Vicki told Wendy to be sure Reuben came with her to work the next day, because she had a surprise for him.

The following morning, when Poppy trotted into 17 Wakely Street, everyone gasped. They leapt out of their chairs and rushed to meet the new doggy face. Everyone took it in turns to stroke her delicate silver fur, and Poppy gave every hand a gentle little lick, her tail wagging shyly behind her.

Then, in a grey-blue flash, Reuben was there! The fun-loving lurcher bounded up to Poppy, who was still feeling a little timid and unsure of what was going on. He wagged his tail furiously and nudged her playfully with his silky muzzle. Poppy seemed to relax as the two sniffed each other and instantly started playing games, chasing each other and rolling around on the floor together, as if they had been friends for years.

'It was great watching them play together,' says Wendy. 'Reuben is so friendly and affectionate, Vicki and I always thought he would get on well with Poppy. But we did not imagine that they would be best friends from the moment they set eyes on each other. It was amazing to see Poppy forget her shyness in an instant, and I felt very proud of Reuben for being such a welcoming gentleman.'

After a few minutes, Reuben took Poppy off to see where she would be sitting. The two lurchers curled up together and that was that.

'Poppy and Reuben love each other dearly,' says Vicki. 'And even though Poppy is actually the bossier one, Reuben has really brought out her mischievous side! It's a bit like Reuben is Poppy's

comedy sidekick. They chase each other around the office, and are much naughtier when they are together. They got Wendy and me into trouble once when they crept into a meeting room and stole a whole big plate of sandwiches!'

Wendy agrees, and says with a grin, 'When Poppy and Reuben are together it's no work, all play, and a bit of sleep thrown in.'

One afternoon in November, Vicki was asked if Poppy would enjoy taking part in the Lord Mayor's Show, a big parade around London with a display of colourful floats. Dogs Trust would be in charge of one of these floats and wanted to take some of their dogs along to show off to the crowd. Thousands of people would be there waving flags and cheering on the procession. It would even be on TV.

Vicky looked at Poppy, who had her nose nuzzled under Reuben's front leg, and decided there could not be a more perfect dog for the job. She was not the sort of girl who would be scared by the noise, she had lots of energy for a long walk through the city, and she was absolutely beautiful. The crowds would love watching her long, elegant body slinking along with the parade.

So Vicky agreed and the day of the Lord Mayor's Show arrived. Vicky had given Poppy a bath with her special doggy shampoo and brushed her coat into a silky silver fluff. She tied a bright yellow Dogs Trust bandana around Poppy's slender neck and stood back to admire her. She looked stunning!

When the two of them arrived where the parade was gathering, there was so much activity it was quite overwhelming, but Poppy soon relaxed and started to enjoy herself. Reuben and some other dogs from the rehoming centres, were there too, so Poppy spent the first hour greeting her friends and making lots of new ones. There were lots of people there, dressed in colourful clothes, and busy tying flowers, flags and banners to their floats.

Soon, the parade was off! Each dog was put on a yellow lead, and had a Dogs Trust walker, who was also dressed smartly in bright yellow and black. When the truck in front began to move, the Dogs Trust float started its engine and began to drive slowly along to where the crowds had gathered. 'How Much Is That Doggy In The Window' started playing and some Dogs Trust staff dressed in dog costumes began dancing on the back of the float, while the dogs and their walkers walked alongside it.

Poppy was delighted to be moving, and sprang into action. When the float went under a bridge and met the crowd on the other side, hundreds of people cheered and waved little flags high in the air. A chorus of 'Aahh!' went up when everyone saw there were real dogs. It was an amazing spectacle, and Poppy walked along proudly, wagging her tail at all the hands that were reaching out over the barriers to stroke her.

It was a long day, but Poppy kept a spring in her

step. Aware she was on display, she behaved beautifully. She made sure her tail kept wagging, and her fuzzy face kept smiling at the crowd throughout the whole day.

'Poppy has done the Lord Mayor's Show for three years running,' says Vicki. 'And all sorts of other walks for Dogs Trust too. She has been all the way to Wales to do a sponsored walk, and she's also done the Great Scottish Walk with Reuben, which is six miles long!

'Her favourite days out at work are the rehoming centre open days, where lots of local families bring their dogs to enjoy games, music, stalls and displays. Poppy is so sociable – she really just loves anything where she meets lots of new doggy faces.'

After that first Lord Mayor's Show, when Poppy had proved what a great sport she was, Dogs Trust staff often came to Vicki's desk to ask if the lovely lurcher would mind helping them with all sorts of things.

'Poppy's been on TV, she's come with me to interviews, and she's really good in photoshoots. She's just so pretty. I don't think a bad photo of her could possibly exist,' says Vicki. 'She has appeared in lots of magazines, and even on a few covers. Dogs Trust like to use her picture lots too, on things like leaflets and posters.'

Pretty Poppy is regularly seen in Dogs Trust's magazine *Wag!*. She has not only been a *Wag!* cover star, but she also has her own column 'Poppy Pops The Question'. She is such a celebrity that Dogs Trust even set up an email address just for Poppy – poppy@dogstrust.org.uk – so her fans can keep in touch and ask her opinions on all things doggy.

Some would say that Poppy is the life and soul of Dogs Trust's London headquarters. And apart from the chief executive, Clarissa, she is certainly its most famous face.

Vicki says proudly, 'It has been four years since Poppy first came to work with me, and now she is just as much a member of Dogs Trust staff as anyone here. She is always particularly excited to come to work on a Monday, and I know that everyone who works with her really looks forward to seeing her after the weekend.'

'Especially Reuben!' says Wendy. 'He knows Mondays are mischief days. There's no guessing what those two will get up to. But they look so cute while they're doing it, and they clearly have so much fun together, that we can't ever be cross with them for long.'

Hubble – the Ugliest Dog in Britain

Wag, wag! Hello readers, Poppy here!

I've been wondering – why are people so obsessed with appearance? We dogs simply can't understand what all the fuss is about.

After all, do you see *us* judging our owners on *their* looks? Do we love them more if they have shiny hair, or white teeth, or a particular body shape? No! We don't care at all! We love people who are kind, loving, dependable and fun, and it doesn't matter one bit if they have wonky faces or wear silly clothes.

Sadly, this is just one of the ways in which dogs are much wiser than people. Not all humans, but lots of them, have just got it wrong! And as a result, the staff here at Dogs Trust often have trouble finding new homes for our less handsome hounds, even though they can have the best personalities and make the loveliest friends. It is something that makes everyone here at Dogs Trust, myself included, feel quite sad.

Sometimes though, we meet a dog whose personality is so sparkling it can outshine even the strangest appearance. Please sit back and enjoy the story of Hubble, a very wonky woofer who was so beautiful on the inside, everyone could see it as clear as day – even people!

Lots of licks,

Pops xxx

I t was a particularly busy autumn Sunday at
Dogs Trust Leeds.

'The reception area was manic,' Amanda, the
rehoming centre manager, remembers. 'Weekends
are always busy because schoolchildren can come
with their parents to meet the dogs, but Sunday
the nineteenth of October was a very busy day
indeed.'

All kinds of noises filled reception – the barking
of excited dogs, the squealing of delighted
children (and grown-ups!) and the jolly hollering
of staff trying to keep everything in order.

One of the members of staff on this particular

Sunday was a lady called Joy, who especially liked working when the rehoming centre was busy. She loved all the hustle and bustle, as long as there were lots more people there to take dogs home than to hand them in.

On days like these, however, when one o'clock arrived, Joy was always more than ready for a break. She looked forward to her quiet lunchtime strolls, with her sandwich and the company of her own four much-loved dogs. They would all bundle into Joy's car. She would drive them to the peaceful woodland a mile or two down the road, where they could all take some time to stretch their legs and enjoy the fresh air together.

On this October Sunday, however, Joy's stroll with her dogs was cut short. They had only taken a few deep breaths of the cool, damp, earthy air, and a few steps towards the entrance to the woods, when a sudden noise made all five of them jump. A distinct rustling sound was coming from just in front of them amongst the trees. Joy looked around and spotted a dark little shape wriggling about on the ground in the autumn leaves. At first, she didn't know what it could be, but she immediately realised that they were not alone!

'All my dogs were still on their leads,' says Joy, 'although they were all pulling at them eagerly – as curious as me to see what or who was lurking in the undergrowth! I could see it was a little black animal, about the size of a young badger, all by himself, tied up to a tree trunk with some rope. There was nobody else around. I took a cautious step forward to get a closer look and that's when the little creature turned his face to us.

'I jumped back in shock at the sight of a small black dog, a terrier, tugging at his rope to come towards us, and baring all his teeth. The little thing looked like he was snarling at me and the dogs – it was quite frightening.'

Luckily, because she loved dogs and had lots of experience looking after them, Joy knew just what to do. She led her own dogs back to the car and shut them inside – their walk would have to wait until she finished work.

'I crept cautiously back to the spot where I had seen the black dog,' says Joy. 'I wanted to take a closer look at him and see if he would be calmer without the other dogs there.

'As I approached, he turned around to look at me, showing his teeth again and looking quite menacing. But there was something peculiar about this little dog. I noticed he was wagging his tail timidly as if to say "I'm friendly really!". I took a few more steps and then I realised that this was no snarling, angry dog. This was a scared but lovely little pooch with a terrible injury on his face. I felt so sorry for him.'

Joy let him sniff her hand and carefully stroked his wiry black fur. The dog wagged his tail and licked Joy's hand, eager to show his delight at being found. After a few minutes of saying hello to each other, Joy untied the dog and walked him to her car. The other four dogs all had their shiny black noses pressed up against the window, ears aloft and eyes wide open, desperate to see what was going on.

Joy had a separate section in her car for her own dogs, so she put her new little friend on a blanket on the back seat, where he would not be overwhelmed by slobbery doggy greetings.

'I will never forget the sight of Joy walking into reception that afternoon,' says Amanda. 'Even though the room was filled with people, dogs and noise, I noticed her straight away, and the little black dog who was tucked under her arm. The poor thing had what looked like a big hole in the middle of his face.'

Joy carried the odd little dog into the back room, moved some things aside on the desk with her spare hand and gently put him down. He immediately wagged his tail good-naturedly and stood still while the two ladies stared at his peculiar little face, and then at each other, and then back at him.

'The poor, poor lad was missing half his nose and the front of his mouth,' says Amanda. 'We had never seen a doggy face like it! All his teeth were sticking out. The two top ones were pointing down, a bit like a vampire, and the two bottom ones were sticking up, a bit like tiny tusks. But his eyes were so shiny and round and innocent, and he was standing there so patiently, that we just wanted to hug him.

'He didn't appear to be in any pain – the wound looked quite old. But when we took a closer look inside his mouth, there was clearly some work to be done. His gums were infected and he would need to have at least a couple of his teeth taken out.'

Amanda and Joy fussed over the little terrier for a few minutes, stroking his fur and accepting friendly licks from his disfigured little mouth. The poor, injured, abandoned dog seemed … happy!

'He did not appear to have a clue how terrible he looked,' says Joy. 'He just wagged his tail and blinked at us, as if to say that he wanted to make new friends he could trust. We tried to show him with cuddles and kind words that we would be delighted to be those friends.'

All the kennels were already full of other dogs waiting for new homes, so they set up a cosy bed for the poor abandoned pooch in the back room. They weren't sure how long he had been tied up in the woods, so they gave him a hearty meal and a big bowl of water, which he wolfed and slurped down gratefully.

Amanda and Joy wondered what sort of life the poor little dog had led. What had happened to make his face so disfigured, and how could anyone abandon him so cruelly? They both promised him that, after all his terrible traumas, they would do everything they could to find him the loving new home he truly deserved.

'The little chap had no collar, and of course his previous owner did not care enough to have had him microchipped,' says Amanda, 'so we had no idea what his name was. But even though we guessed he was about eight years old, we thought it was time for a brand new start. Halloween was just a few days away, and we joked that because of his unusual looks he should have a spooky name!

'Joy thought of the witches' rhyme "Hubble bubble, toil and trouble". The name Hubble seemed to suit our adorable little dog perfectly, because he had certainly been through a great deal of toil and trouble in his life.'

Whatever that toil and trouble was must have been very distressing, and Hubble's terrible wound must have been very painful for him at the time. Amanda thinks the injury could have come from a fight with a badger. 'It would be very unusual for a dog to want to fight with a badger,' she says, 'so I think it's more likely that a human made him do it. Even though badgers are timid creatures, they have enormous, powerful claws, which can do terrible damage when they are defending themselves. Sadly, there are some very nasty people out there who enjoy making peaceful creatures fight for their lives.'

Very quickly, it also became clear that while little Hubble was adorable and friendly to every human he met, he was scared stiff around all other dogs. 'This was another clue that he was made to fight with other animals,' Amanda says, sadly. 'Hubble has such a kind and loving personality that something very terrifying must have happened to make him feel so scared around his fellow dogs. But we probably won't ever know for certain exactly what those terrible things were.'

A few days went by at Dogs Trust Leeds. Hubble had been to see the vet, who carefully cleaned up his teeth, took out the ones that had gone bad and gave him medicine for the infection. The vet gave him lots of other tests, and said whatever Hubble had been through had sadly also made him a little bit deaf. But apart from that he was a fit and healthy boy, with so much to offer an owner who understood how special he was.

Hubble was still sleeping in the back room at

night, and during the day he would sit behind reception watching all the goings-on at Dogs Trust. He loved all the bustle and commotion. And as long as there was a desk between him and any other dogs that came into the room, he felt completely safe.

'He was so good,' says Amanda, smiling. 'He loved all the attention. Whoever was working as receptionist would have to have Hubble sitting on their knee – he insisted on it! No one minded because every member of staff just adored him. And everyone who came through the doors who had not met him before would make a comment when they saw his strange little face popping up from behind the desk.'

One day, Amanda was standing behind reception with little Hubble sitting on the floor looking up at her, gently wagging his soft, bristly black tail. She took a doggy treat out of a bag and passed it to him. The delighted dog crunched on it eagerly, blissfully unaware as usual that crumbs were dropping out of either side of his wonky little mouth. Amanda's heart leapt with fondness for this goofy but gorgeous dog.

She suddenly realised that Hubble's new owner should be someone who would not just overlook his funny face, but who would love him even more because of it – just like she did. Hubble was such a special dog that he deserved a truly special owner. Right then, Amanda made a decision. She would start a nationwide search.

Katy was sitting at her desk at Dogs Trust HQ in London, trying to concentrate on her work as Reuben and Poppy chased each other around the office. Even though both dogs were very fast, Poppy always beat Reuben around corners, and today's race was no different. Katy was laughing at the two speeding lurchers as her phone rang. It was Amanda, claiming that she believed 'the most unusual dog in Britain' was living behind reception at Dogs Trust Leeds!

Amanda emailed Hubble's photo to Katy, and

explained how he had been cruelly abandoned in the woods. Katy agreed that they must do everything possible to find this poor pooch the caring new owner he deserved. She said Hubble was certainly the strangest looking dog she had ever seen, and immediately set to work calling all the newspapers to tell them his story.

Later that day, newspaper printing presses across the country clanked, then they clunked, and then they started whirring. They whirred all through the night, and by morning, when people all across the UK were waking up and opening their newspapers, Hubble was a star!

Under the headline 'Britain's Ugliest Dog', a big photograph of the toothy terrier stared out from the page. It was a lovely picture. Of course, Hubble's face looked terribly disfigured, but his black fur, flecked with grey around his little face, looked lovely and his shiny round eyes looked kind and gentle.

Everyone was touched by Hubble's story. All

day, in homes, schools and offices, people were talking about the poor little dog with the ugly face who had been found tied up in the woods.

'For the next few days we were overwhelmed with phone calls,' says Amanda. 'So many people saw the beautiful character shining through Hubble's strange little face, and desperately wanted to give him a home.'

Hubble was, by now, a true celebrity. A lady

called Sarah from Dogs Trust Leeds had taken him to London, where the two of them appeared on television to tell his story. Hubble adored all the attention and, even now that he was famous, he was as charming and affectionate as always. Everyone he met fell in love with him – even the TV presenters said they wanted to take him home!

The telephone rang and rang at Dogs Trust Leeds. Amanda says, 'Can you believe we had over 500 calls. Even some from America and Switzerland. It was wonderful that so many people saw past Hubble's looks and wanted to adopt him. It meant we could choose exactly the right home for him, where we knew he could spend his life being blissfully happy and loved.'

While all this commotion was going on in Leeds, it was a normal day for Judith, who was sitting at her desk at work in County Durham. 'My friend at work called me over to look at her computer screen,' says Judith. 'She had been looking at the

Dogs Trust website and found a picture of a poor little dog called Hubble who was lovely but had a terrible injury on his face. As soon as I saw him, I felt so sad for him and I fell in love with the dear little thing instantly.

'When I got home from work, I went online to look at Hubble again. I thought Dogs Trust would be having a terrible time trying to find a home for a dog with such an odd face. I had no idea he was an international superstar! And I'm so, so pleased I didn't. If I had known over 500 people wanted to adopt him, it's possible I wouldn't have jumped in the car and driven all the way to Leeds to say I wanted him too!'

When Judith and her husband Edward got to the rehoming centre and met Hubble, they were overwhelmed with affection for the lovely chap. Amanda asked them if they would like to take him out for a walk so they could get to know him a bit better.

'I couldn't take my eyes off him. I just kept

staring at him while he was scampering about –
he was so wonderful!' Judith says. 'When we came
back from our walk together, I told Amanda we
had decided that we desperately wanted him.
That's when she told us that Hubble was actually
a famous celebrity! Our hearts sank when she
explained that hundreds of other people wanted
him too.'

Judith and Edward drove all the way home and
spent the next few days nervously waiting for
news of Hubble. Now that they had met and
fallen in love with him, they would be devastated
if he couldn't come to live with them.

Meanwhile, everyone at Dogs Trust Leeds was
frantically trying to match Hubble with his perfect
new home. 'Lots of people had other dogs, so we
crossed them off our list,' says Amanda. 'We wanted
to find a home where Hubble would feel
completely safe, without any other pets, so he could
have all the love and cuddles for himself. We were
also looking for people who could spend lots of

time with him. He'd been through so much in his eight years, now he deserved to be spoilt rotten!'

After a long and exhausting search, when Amanda was finally sure she had found Hubble's perfect new owner, Judith's phone rang. 'I knew that Judith, Edward and Hubble would have a wonderful life together,' says Amanda. 'Judith and Edward had lots of experience looking after dogs, but their last dog Hector, a wonderful Yorkshire Terrier with a huge personality, had passed away a few months before. They both work, but on different days, so there would always be someone at home to keep Hubble company. And when they met him, I could see they clearly all adored each other!'

'We just couldn't believe it when Amanda told us,' says Judith. 'We were so happy we had been chosen from all those people. And now that we all live together, all three of us are happy! Hubble is just fabulous. When Edward and I adopted him, we wanted to give him a happy, secure, stable home where he could relax and be himself.

'He knows this is his home now. He's so affectionate and he makes a huge fuss of any visitors who come round, so all our friends think he's wonderful. He loves being in the garden and we walk him three times a day, which has made us much fitter too.

'Of course, we don't know what happened to Hubble in his past, but I know he had some horrible experiences that he's still recovering from. Other dogs, especially large black ones, completely terrify him and whenever he sees one, he looks up at me for reassurance. I'm happy he trusts me and knows I will take care of him, but looking down at his scared little face breaks my heart.

'I've taught our lovely Hubble a little bit of sign language because of his deafness. I have never taught a dog that way before, so we are learning together! And Hubble is learning to play and have proper doggy fun too. I suppose there wasn't

much fun in his old life, so I love it when I see him running about without a care in the world. The other day he scampered proudly into the kitchen with a wedge of apple in his mouth, looking like a big green grin! He is always doing things that make us smile. We just love him to bits.

'Although he's naturally such a happy little dog, and he is getting more confident every single day, sometimes at home he has sad days too. I can tell if he's feeling insecure, because he will get his toy hedgehog, his bone, and one of our shoes if he can find one, and he'll curl up quietly with them all in his bed.

'But Hubble is an absolute joy in our lives. I am so proud to be his owner. Sometimes, when I'm walking him, people stare or give us funny looks. I don't mind though. I just walk past and smile to myself, knowing that if they met him properly, they would fall in love too, and see straight away that Hubble is the most beautiful dog in the world!'

Cracker's Explosive Tale

Wag, wag! Lick! Hi again, readers.

I do hope you've been enjoying these doggy tales so far. By now, I'm sure you'll agree that dogs make the best pets in the world. It's important for humans to know, however, that we dogs can be even more than just pets.

Now I know what you're thinking. What job could possibly be better than being a pet dog? What greater responsibility could there be than providing people with love, comfort, laughter and fun? Surely no duty is more important than laying a furry chin on the knee of someone sad, or asking someone who feels lonely to play with you?

However, if you can believe it, some dogs do even more valuable work than this. Some help thousands of people every day. And among the many amazing talents we dogs can have, some are able to solve crimes, catch criminals and even save lives.

This next story is about a fantastic dog I know, called Cracker. When he was just a puppy, he faced one of the biggest challenges that life can throw at a dog – being abandoned. But just like great humans, great dogs don't let anything get in the way of their destiny. And now thousands of people in London rely on dogs like Cracker to keep them safe by doing some of the most important jobs in the country.

Please allow me to present Cracker, and the truly cracking tale that makes me feel especially proud to be a dog.

Woof woof, with lots of love,

Poppy xxx

Most police constables greet their workmates with a nod of the head, a professional, important-sounding 'All right, mate', and sometimes a sturdy handshake. Some also like to include a slight twinkle in the eye, or allow the hint of a smile to curl in the very corners of the mouth.

Most police constables certainly do not bound up to each other with their mouths open and tongues hanging out. They do not usually leap into the air and throw their arms open to each other, and their eyes do not commonly shine bright with sheer joy and unconditional love.

But Cracker isn't your usual policeman, and he

most certainly doesn't play by the usual rules where greeting is concerned. When Cracker is pleased to see his work partner PC Turner, he is very, very proud to show it. He jumps up eagerly, putting his large, soft paws on PC Turner's ironed shirt to get as close as possible to his much-loved workmate's face. He wags his heavy tail in big, wide sweeps so its long fur flows behind it, and his shiny brown eyes are full of unmistakable love for PC Turner.

If Cracker were a human, PC Turner would probably ask him quietly to control these embarrassing displays of affection. But as it is, PC Turner leans down happily and ruffles the dog's velvety fur with both hands. With a wide smile, he takes a little bone-shaped treat out of his pocket and hands it to his overjoyed friend. And, actually, it is clear that PC Turner is delighted to see Cracker too.

Despite their unusual greeting habits, when the pair get to work they are a very highly-skilled team. With PC Turner's expert brain and Cracker's expert nose, the two of them work hard every day keeping London's streets, buses and trains safe for everyone.

Watching Cracker at work, you would think that the keen and energetic springer spaniel had been born and bred in the police force. You would never guess that just four months ago, he was a young dog with no home and no owner, brought like so many others to the door of Dogs Trust Shoreham …

'It was in late December when we first met Cracker,' says Tracey, manager of Dogs Trust Shoreham. 'We have been repeating our slogan "A dog is for life, not just for Christmas" for over thirty years now, but so many dogs are still abandoned around Christmas time. It's terribly sad, because Christmas is supposed to be the time when everyone is especially kind and generous to each other.'

It was seven o'clock in the morning and Tracey

was heading to Dogs Trust Shoreham to start the day's work, shivering in the chilly December air.

She shuffled up the path as fast as she could in her big boots and warm coat, fumbling with her chunky bunch of keys. She was eager to get into the warmth as quickly as possible, but just as she was turning her key in the lock, she heard a little yelp.

She looked around, then down at the ground, and in the corner of the entrance-way, someone had left a big cardboard box. The box hadn't been there when Tracey left work the night before. It was wrapped in shiny Christmas paper, but its top flaps were not secured.

She walked over to the giant present and lifted the flaps. 'By this time, I knew what was going to be inside,' she says, 'because both the cardboard flaps were all wet at the edges and I could see they'd been chewed by nervous doggy teeth.'

Inside the big box, staring up at her, was a young auburn and white springer spaniel. He was looking very worried. 'The poor dog had only been given a thin little blanket to sit on and was clearly so cold,' says Tracey. 'Even though whoever left him there cared enough to bring him to Dogs Trust, I felt cross that they'd only given him a tiny rag for warmth. It had been so cold the night before, it must have been awful for him. I couldn't wait to get him inside.'

She carefully lifted the shivering young dog out of the box, finished unlocking the front door and took him into reception. Once he had warmed up and Tracey had given him some food and water, the young spaniel seemed to forget his nerves. He began to pad around reception, his little claws *tip-tap-tapping* on the floor as he scampered around. He snuffled inquisitively around every corner of the room, wagging his tail and occasionally stopping for a pat from Tracey.

'He was just such a *busy* little dog,' says Tracey. 'From the very moment he came inside that day, he was *doing* things. He was full of energy and interested in everything around him – always checking things out and constantly playing with the toys. His tennis ball was his very favourite thing. I hardly ever saw him lying down, like some of our other dogs who like to take life a little bit slower!

'Of course, he came with no name, but we thought Cracker seemed to suit him well. He was definitely a cracking little dog, and finding him inside that box made me think of the surprise inside a Christmas cracker!'

Young Cracker settled into rehoming centre life very quickly. He was introduced to his kennel-mate Marion, a tiny, friendly Yorkshire terrier cross whom he immediately adored. After an accident she had as a puppy, little Marion could only see out of one eye. This made her a bit slower and clumsier when it came to playing Cracker's games, but she joined in happily nonetheless.

Tracey and the other rehoming centre staff were fascinated by Cracker. 'He seemed incredibly intelligent and extremely eager to please,' says Tracey. 'He picked things up very, very quickly –

games we introduced him to, instructions we gave him – anything we asked of him, really. We would only have to show him how to do something once or twice and then the next time he would do it by himself. He was a remarkably clever dog.'

One morning, two weeks after Cracker's arrival at Dogs Trust, Cracker and Marion's canine carer Jemma went into their kennel. First, she dislodged little Marion, who had got herself entangled in a blanket while playing one of Cracker's games. Then she put the dogs' leads on to take them out for their afternoon walk.

Out in the cold December air, as she watched Cracker scampering around busily in the bushes, Jemma wondered to herself if he had what it took to become a *police dog*. Her boyfriend Chris was a policeman, and had told her that the police were always on the lookout for intelligent, energetic doggy recruits. 'Cracker had so much energy it was ridiculous!' says Jemma. 'I started to wonder if he would find enough to satisfy all that curiosity

Poppy the Dogs Trust Dog

in a normal home. Perhaps it would be good for him to have a job that he could focus on? Maybe all that intelligence and get-up-and-go could be developed and even used to help people?'

That evening, Jemma told Chris about the amazingly bright dog who had been abandoned in a Christmas box on the doorstep. He said he would love to come and meet Cracker to see if he thought he was cut out for the police force, and did so the very next day.

In their big winter coats, Tracey, Jemma and Chris took Cracker into the rehoming centre's doggy exercise area to test out his skills. Chris used a tennis ball as Cracker's reward for doing the exercises (which was easy as tennis balls were Cracker's favourite thing anyway). He was astonished by how quickly the sparky young spaniel picked things up.

First of all Chris tried some retrieving exercises, which Cracker grasped beautifully. Excitedly, he watched for where Chris was going to throw the ball. Straight away, he dashed after it, picked it up and trotted back with it. He then dropped it at Chris's feet for him to throw again.

After that, Chris tried hiding the tennis ball around the exercise area and asking the young dog to find it. He wanted to see just how much Cracker wanted to get the ball back, and how long and hard he would search for it.

With his sensitive brown nose to the ground and his tail wagging behind him in concentration, Cracker searched every corner of the area. Time after time, he did not stop searching until he found his ball.

'Chris was amazed,' says Jemma. 'For Cracker, finding that tennis ball was clearly more serious than just a game. And he used his nose to find it. Some dogs find things by *looking* at the possible places it could be. Others *remember* where it has been in the past and go there first. Cracker *sniffed out* the ball, and that's just the sort of dog the police want.'

Everyone knew right then that even though

Cracker hadn't had proper training yet, he was a perfect trainee, and had everything he could possibly need to work with the police. Chris went back to the station and told his workmates all about the fantastic dog he had met.

The next day, a policeman phoned Tracey and they agreed that Cracker would start the next police dog training course in early January. Everything was decided – he would be rehomed to a nice dog-loving police officer, who he would live, train and play with. He would spend Christmas getting to know his new owner and then they would start work together.

However, as can often be the case with a perfect plan, there was a slight hiccup. A slight hiccup, then a little cough, then a bigger cough …

Poor Cracker had developed a nasty case of kennel cough and the vet thought it would be better for him to stay where he was until he got better.

So Cracker spent Christmas at Dogs Trust

Shoreham, which is not such a bad place to be on Christmas Day. 'Because we get so many donations from people throughout the year, we save up lots of them for Christmas time,' says Jemma. 'Then on Christmas Eve, Christmas Day and Boxing Day we share all the goodies out amongst the dogs. They each have their own little stocking.

'They have a really lovely time, and it's fun for the staff too. We can always hear lots of noise coming from the kennel blocks as all the dogs are playing with their squeaky toys. For us, that's the sound of Christmas – the sound of all the dogs playing in their kennels and enjoying themselves.'

Lots of the staff and dogs, including Tracey, Jemma, Cracker and Marion, went out for a lovely long walk across the fields on Christmas Day. 'It was great – that huge Christmas Day walk is always loads of fun,' says Jemma. 'And afterwards, when we got back, all the dogs were so sleepy that they completely crashed out in their kennels! All the excited noises from the dogs playing with their new toys had quietened down to just a few lazy squeaks.'

After Christmas, and when his cough had got better, Cracker's big day finally arrived. As tiny Marion looked on sadly, Cracker was taken out of his kennel with pats and treats from a policeman, and taken away to start his training.

At last, Cracker's career had begun.

In the large introduction room at the police dog training centre in Surrey, lots of policemen and their doggy partners were waiting for the training to start. The eight-week course would be hard work, but plenty of fun as well. Just like Cracker, all the dogs had been specially selected for their brightness and eagerness to play and learn. Many of them were rescue dogs too.

In the big noisy room, there was just one policeman who was standing on his own in his crisp black uniform, looking around expectantly for his new canine partner. Just as Cracker was led

in through the door, PC Turner spotted him and dashed over to the lovely, glossy springer spaniel.

As always, Cracker was enthusiastic and friendly when they met, sniffing and wagging his big tail at the kindly stranger. PC Turner welcomed his cheerful dog with pats and treats. He had been told Cracker was lovely, and he was especially delighted that the two of them seemed to hit it off straight away. It was a relief because their training together would start that very afternoon.

'As soon as we started I could see that Cracker

was fun, bouncy and very keen to work,' says PC Turner. 'We had loads of fun together, and he was an absolute joy to work with.

'In the first few days, we worked on Cracker's great skill for finding things, using his ball as a reward when he recognised certain scents.

'As the weeks went on, we started to introduce Cracker to different smells. Dogs have very sensitive noses and can smell things in the air that humans could never smell. There are dogs who are trained to sniff out illegal drugs, or large amounts of cash — lots of different things. We wanted to train Cracker to be an explosives dog, so if there were any bombs in a place we asked him to search, he would find them with his nose and then tell us.'

The pair learned how to enter and leave a dangerous building together, and how to search it properly and thoroughly. They also practised how to find explosives safely in all sorts of different places.

'Cracker's brilliant, and really funny to watch

when he finds something,' PC Turner says with a smile. 'Without touching the place where we have hidden the smell, he will put his nose next to it. He will keep his head completely still – steady as a rock. Then his tail wags furiously, in such huge movements that his whole body wags with it!'

Always using Cracker's tennis ball as a reward, PC Turner guided Cracker through the whole eight weeks of training, and the two of them passed the course with flying colours.

Now that they're qualified, PC Turner and Cracker are licensed to work together for the British Transport Police Dog Section. They work in train and underground stations, on the streets, and anywhere else they are sent in the capital. PC Turner is not allowed to work with any other dog and Cracker cannot work with any other handler, so the two of them spend every working day together patrolling London and keeping it safe from explosives, and Cracker lives with PC Turner too.

Everyone who knows Cracker agrees that he

Poppy the
Dogs Trust dog

Poppy the shoe-sized pup

© Pat Doyle

Poppy the model dog!

Hubble with author, Sophia, and Dogs Trust
press officer, Krystyna

Hubble with his
new owner Judith

Cracker and
P.C. Turner on
the beat

Cracker puts his nose
to work

© Stanford Photographic

was made for a career in the police force. PC Turner says that in the mornings, as the two of them are getting ready to start their day, Cracker always checks to see if his owner is wearing his work clothes. If he sees the starchy black uniform and the big black boots, the dog's tail starts wagging frantically and he leaps about with joy, knowing they will be going to work that day.

Cracker has fun on his days off too, romping around in the garden with PC Turner's other dog, a fluffy collie-cross called Jacko. The two dogs have only lived together for four months, but they have become the very best of friends.

'Those two love playing a game of tug-o-war together,' says PC Turner. 'It's one game that Cracker really enjoys but doesn't get to play at work. He is less skilled at that particular game than Jacko though, who likes to let go of the toy just as Cracker is standing with his back to the garden pond. Cracker goes flying backwards and gets a big shock when he suddenly finds himself plunged into freezing cold water!'

PC Turner thinks it's important that Cracker enjoys his time off as well as his days at work. 'I have to make sure he stays interested in his job,' says the proud policeman, 'so he has to have other sorts of fun too, including good old-fashioned doggy fun.

'And even though nothing can beat the joy of playing fetch with his tennis ball, I am delighted to say that Cracker's next favourite toy is most definitely … Jacko!'

Weasel, Earless but Fearless

Hello readers, it's me again! Wag, wag!

As I was snuffling through a colleague's waste-paper bin yesterday, I came across an old newspaper article about a dog called Weasel. He looked so strange and cute in the photograph that I just had to tell you his story.

Like most pups, Weasel was probably born a happy, secure and energetic little animal, safe with his mother and the rest of his litter. Most likely, he didn't think he was different at all! Unfortunately, his owners did not agree. What they saw was a deformed puppy who lacked a very important feature.

Weasel had no ears.

Can you imagine what it would be like to live without ears? You humans couldn't wear earphones,

73

earrings, and certainly not glasses. Not to mention the fact that you wouldn't be able to hear properly! I find it particularly difficult to imagine being earless because, as you know, my own ears are one of my prettiest features. And they're not just delicate, silver and elegantly floaty, but they work extremely well too. In fact, I can hear a lot better than my human friends.

So, being born with no ears meant Weasel was a little dog with a big problem. Not only was he lacking the sharp hearing that is important to a dog, but the poor chap looked so strange with his tiny earless head that his owners were ashamed of him. And, even though he was just a defenceless puppy in need of help, they sent him out to face the world on his own. It's very unfair, but there are some people who will only love us dogs as long as we don't give them any problems. I mean, as if all people are perfect!

So Weasel's story could have ended right there, when he was thrown out alone into the street. He was far too young to survive without his family. But read on and you will learn about all the travels and adventures that have made brave Weasel into the amazing dog that he is today.

Love and wags,

Pops xxx

It was a cold winter morning when a man walked into Bridgend police station, carrying a tiny, shivering bundle. Nestling in the crook of the man's arm was a puppy, only a few weeks old, that he had found huddled in the street. Hungry, afraid and desperate for warmth, the pup used his tiny paws to snuggle deeper into the man's warm winter coat.

Looking down fondly at the little wriggling thing, the man explained sadly that he couldn't just walk past a creature in need. He said he loved dogs and wished he could keep this one, but he couldn't take on the responsibility of dog ownership at the moment. Nodding understandingly, the police officer said he had done the right thing bringing the dog to the station. He reached to pull down a folder marked 'Strays' from a shelf, and then suddenly caught a proper view of the little puppy. He stopped what he was doing, leant over the desk and stared in amazement.

The police officer had seen many lost and abandoned dogs at the station, but this one was by far the strangest. Although the puppy was still very small, it was clear to see that something important was missing from his little furry head.

This puppy had no ears!

As astounded as he was, the policeman still had to follow the proper procedures, so he filled out the forms and telephoned to have the poor little creature taken to the local dog pound.

The dog pound can sometimes be a happy place where lost dogs are reunited with their worried owners. But often the owners never come, and, as everyone expected, no one came for the earless puppy.

Luckily, Beverley, manager of Dogs Trust Bridgend, heard about the peculiar pooch and went to see him. Like all the charity's rehoming centre managers, Beverley works closely with the local pounds and helps needy dogs there wherever she can. Gazing at the tiny pup, she saw that he was mostly border terrier — a breed of usually brave and hardy little dogs. But this poor chap was frightened and cowering in the corner of his kennel. Since he had no ears and seemed so scared and unhappy, Beverley thought he must be deaf. This dog needed special care, so she took him to the rehoming centre, where he became the centre of attention straight away.

'When I brought him back to the centre, everyone gathered around to see the unusual new arrival,' says Beverley. 'The first time I saw his tiny earless head, I thought "He looks just like a little weasel!" And when I showed him to the other staff, everyone agreed! So that was how Weasel got his name.'

Because of his lack of ears, little Weasel took several months to get used to life in the kennels. Sudden movements can startle and frighten deaf dogs, because they often don't understand what is happening around them. For instance, they can't hear people leaving, and are upset when they discover that someone they thought was there has gone.

The staff found little Weasel's condition heartbreaking. They soon found that he could hear certain sounds, but he was very nervous and would jump at a sudden noise, as if he didn't know where it had come from.

Everyone at the rehoming centre gave the earless pup plenty of love and attention, stroking and touching him a lot to reassure him that he was safe. They took him out of his kennel often and let him spend lots of time running free in the courtyard.

Slowly but surely, young Weasel began to feel secure. And as his confidence grew, he started to show what he was made of. Border terriers are active little dogs, full of fun and mischief, and Weasel was no exception. He began socialising with the other dogs and getting up to all sorts of tricks. His carers made sure that he had plenty of time outside, and he loved to run in the large field next to the centre. 'He really covered some ground out there!' says Beverley. 'We would take him to the field and just let him go for the burn! And he loved it – he adored the freedom and the fresh air.'

True to his terrier nature, Weasel was a busy little dog in lots of ways, and he was looking for something new to try. He was bright, and soon he began to learn a kind of doggy sign language to help him understand what his carers were saying to him, which he picked up with great enthusiasm. Watching attentively, if he saw someone extend their hand, palm down, and lower it slowly, he knew that meant sit. If they patted their thighs with both hands, that meant come here. The little dog clearly wanted to understand what was going on and was doing all he could, despite his lack of ears.

When the vet came to see Weasel, he declared that in all his years of experience, he had never seen an earless dog! He was a truly remarkable case, and had been born with a layer of skin that completely covered where his ears should have been. After examining Weasel thoroughly, however, the vet was surprised to find that the dog's inner ears were intact. He could probably hear muffled sounds as if he were swimming deep under water, but if the vet could open up his ear holes, the chances were that Weasel would be able to hear as well as any other dog.

Soon, the unique puppy was causing quite a stir. Newspaper reporters heard about him and came from miles around to see him. Adorable photographs were printed alongside his story in the papers. Weasel was a beautiful little dog with wiry black and brown fur and big trusting eyes. And somehow, his lack of ears made him look even more adorable. Hundreds of people who wanted to give him a new home contacted Dogs Trust. One admirer even knitted him a hat and posted it to the Bridgend rehoming centre. 'It's such a cold winter – this is to keep Weasel's head warm!' said the note. And, when he went on

breakfast television, all the presenters fell in love with him too.

Weasel had become a proper celebrity, and people came from as far as Japan wanting to film his story.

Because he had become such a brave and happy little dog, the vet decided that Weasel could cope with the operation that would make him able to hear. First, he needed hearing tests at a specialist clinic in faraway Southampton. Beverley, who had become the plucky little dog's best friend, took him on the long train journey.

'When we set off, I quickly realised that the whole country seemed to know about Weasel,' says Beverley with a smile. 'While we were walking around Southampton, we were constantly being stopped. People rushed up to us all the time, saying they had seen him on TV or in the newspaper, asking how he was and wanting to stroke him. Even on the train, when he would mischievously stick his little head out of the carrier basket, people would say, "That's Weasel! You know – the dog from the papers!" It was an extraordinary experience.'

All this could have overwhelmed a young and almost deaf dog who had started life abandoned and hungry on the street, but young Weasel took everything in his stride. Nothing was a problem for him – the train and car journeys, the curiosity from fans on the street, even staying overnight in a hotel. He loved all the attention.

After the big trip to Southampton, Weasel arrived back at Dogs Trust Bridgend even more confident and outgoing than when he'd left. And all the experts now agreed – the operation to open up Weasel's ears should go ahead. It would be done at Bristol University.

So, safe in the knowledge that he enjoyed a little adventure and would be beautifully behaved, Beverley and Weasel set off to Bristol. And once again he showed the world he was a small dog with a huge personality. He was so famous now that he attracted even more attention in Bristol than he had in Southampton. He was a great hit with everyone – especially the young student vets at the university who were lucky enough to spend lots of time with him.

The time for the operation had arrived. Beverley had to leave her earless friend inside the vet's operating room and go back to the rehoming centre because the little patient would have to stay there overnight. As she left the room, she turned to look at little Weasel, who seemed smaller and more helpless than ever sitting on the operating table. At that moment, Beverley, who had cared for thousands of stray and abandoned dogs since she had been manager of Dogs Trust, realised how attached she had become to this little dog in particular.

All sorts of things were going through her mind as she made the journey back to Bridgend. The experts had assured her that the operation was low-risk and that Weasel would be fine, but what if he wasn't? What if the operation went wrong and he lost his hearing completely? Would that be better or worse than hearing only muffled sounds and being constantly startled all the time?

But Beverley need not have worried because the vets were right, and the next day they called to say that the operation had been a success. And for the first time Weasel could hear properly. 'It was amazing for him,' says Beverley. 'When I went to pick him up I could tell he suddenly knew what was happening around him. He adjusted to the change straight away. He seemed so much happier because he wasn't surrounded by strange and frightening vibrations anymore, but clear sounds that he could identify. When we went back to the centre, he could hear the snuffles and barks of other dogs and the voices of all his human friends. It truly was a new start for him.'

Weasel stayed on at the rehoming centre for a few more months. In that time, he got used to being a normal dog – having fun with all his human and canine chums, and hearing all sorts of exciting new sounds. People from all over the world wanted to know about his progress and sent him letters, cards, pictures and presents.

Among all the thousands of people who fell in love with Weasel in those months was Carolyn, a fitness instructor and dog-lover from North Wales. 'It was just a normal day at the gym when I first saw the funny little earless dog on the television,' says Carolyn. 'I was so touched by Weasel's story that I called Dogs Trust to ask about him. And from then on, I phoned every week, sometimes twice, to see how he was getting on.'

Now he was happy, confident and with his hearing intact, Weasel was finally ready to find a home. Beverley was determined that he should be with someone who could give him lots of love and attention. For hours, she sorted through the letters, emails, and application forms from all the people who wanted him. But throughout the process, her thoughts kept returning to Carolyn. 'She just seemed so perfect,' Beverley says. 'Because Weasel had had such a difficult life, we felt he should be with someone who would have a lot of time and patience. Because she called all the time to ask after him, we knew she had lots of love to give him. Also, he needed an energetic and lively owner because he was such a busy, active little thing. I became more and more convinced that Carolyn was the one.'

Mold, about four hours away from Bridgend,

was the village where Carolyn lived. She and her husband owned the gym just half a mile from their house. They both worked there but in two shifts, so there was always someone at home. They lived a very active lifestyle and loved to run, sometimes ten miles a day, with their beautiful female patterdale Gibson running along beside them.

'I hadn't actually thought of applying to rehome Weasel!' says Carolyn. 'When I saw him on television, I just thought how beautiful he was. His funny little earless head made him even more endearing. I went online to make a donation to Dogs Trust and there he was again. There was an invitation to fill in a form if I was interested in rehoming him, but I knew that because he was such a celebrity, hundreds of people would want him, and I really didn't think I would stand a chance.'

However one day, Carolyn was working at her gym when she had a telephone call from Beverley.

She asked Carolyn to come and meet Weasel in person. 'I was so excited but I didn't want to get my hopes up,' says Carolyn. 'Also, it was an eight-hour trip to the rehoming centre and back. I couldn't go without Gibson, but the journey would be hard on her. Beverley encouraged us to come and meet Weasel though, and said our family would be perfect for him.

'I'll never forget the first time we saw him. Weasel came rushing up to us wagging his tail and I cried! He was so excited he actually piddled! He got on well with Gibson. All three of us fell in love with him, actually, so it was perfect. In a matter of minutes, we all agreed that he should come and live with us.'

Soon Weasel and Beverley made their last and happiest journey together to Weasel's new home and his excited new family. As usual, by the time they arrived, the news had got out. Beverley and Weasel were used to it by now though! The headline on the newspaper stands stated boldly

'No-eared dog comes to Mold'. Local press reporters and photographers were gathered at Carolyn's gate, snapping pictures and making all sorts of noise calling out questions to Carolyn and Beverley.

'It was so funny,' laughs Beverley. 'It was like being followed by the paparazzi. Now I know what it's like to be Madonna! I've never known such a small dog to cause such a stir, and Weasel coped splendidly. And though of course I was pleased that my earless friend had a new home to start another chapter in his life, I knew I would really miss him.'

At first things didn't go as smoothly as everyone hoped in Weasel's new home. Although they got on well at their first meeting, Gibson decided she was not happy to have a new member in her family. Meeting a dog for a couple of hours was a very different thing to having a new doggy housemate, according to Gibson! She often growled and snapped at Weasel and for some time there was tension and unhappiness in the home.

Finally, Carolyn went to a dog psychiatrist for advice. He pointed out that Gibson was feeling threatened by the new arrival. When she was told off for snapping, she felt even more unhappy and blamed Weasel. Somehow, they had to break the pattern. Although it seemed strange, the psychiatrist told Carolyn to take Weasel from the room when he was attacked and to make a fuss of Gibson instead. That way, she was letting the grumpy dog know that she was still secure and loved. 'I felt so guilty making Weasel leave the room when he hadn't done anything wrong,' says Carolyn, 'but the psychiatrist was right. Gibson was just feeling jealous and thinking that Weasel was our new favourite. Once she realised we still loved her as much as ever, she accepted Weasel and now the pair are good friends.

'Actually, they love each other,' Carolyn continues, fondly. 'They snuggle up together and she licks him. And sometimes Weasel lies on the floor in front of the fire and Gibson lies beside him with her front leg over him, like she's actually cuddling him! Weasel loves watching television too. He sits behind me on the sofa, and puts his head on my shoulder while he's watching the screen and listening to the sounds. He must be so pleased he can hear properly now because everyone knows TV is much, much better with sound!'

Weasel and Gibson share a common interest in socks, which they have developed into a sort of game. Both dogs wait for Carolyn to take the laundry out of the machine, hoping for a falling sock. Then they pounce and the dog who manages to catch it will whisk it away for a good chewing, then playfully guard it from the other. The family dogs are blissfully happy together now. There is always something to do, lots of fun and affection, the odd sock here and there, and of course those wonderful long runs in the countryside. What dog could wish for more?

So, Weasel has come a long way in his short life. He was abandoned in the street one cold winter morning. He spent sad, lonely days at the dog pound until Beverley came to rescue him. He faced long journeys and he survived the operation that enabled him to hear normally. Now he lives a happy life with a family that loves him – love

Poppy the Dogs Trust Dog

that he eagerly returns. And through it all Weasel has remained the brave little dog that he is. To this day, the whole village is proud of their local celebrity dog: Weasel – *earless but fearless*.

Doctor Morris – Therapist Dog

Hi again readers.

Lick, lick!

You know, we all have our challenges in life – humans and dogs alike. Some of us just have the usual ups and downs – for instance, sometimes at work Reuben manages to get more treats than me, and it's a proper *nightmare* when I forget where I've buried my bone. But some others have to go through extraordinary and terrible hardships, like being abandoned or coming down with a serious illness.

For dogs at least, there are two types of challenge. There are those where we are alone and uncared for in the world, and those where we have the support of a loving owner. What I have learned while working at Dogs Trust is if dogs face their challenges alone, life can really get them down. They may not even survive. But with the extra strength of someone who loves them, they can triumph over even the most terrible difficulties.

Take Morris, a dog who had so much love from his owner, he not only used it to overcome his own terrible troubles, he had enough left over to help others with theirs too!

Nuzzles,
Poppy xxx

Jacqui had always wanted a dog. When she was little, she loved visiting friends who had dogs. She would make sure the dog was involved in all the games they played in the garden, and if they went out anywhere, she would beg for the dog to come with them. She loved the happiness and energy that dogs brought to all activities – even things that were usually boring, like car trips or the walk to the corner shop – and noticed how much more fun life was with a dog.

But throughout her childhood, Jacqui never had a canine companion of her own. Every time she visited a house with a dog, or even just saw one walking down the road with its owner, she felt a little pang of jealousy. She didn't just want a dog for the fun bits, like the games and the cuddles. She would be proud to take on all the other responsibilities that came with caring for a dog too – like grooming its coat, taking it for walks every day, and even picking up its poop!

Jacqui knew that she would be a fantastic dog owner, and made a firm promise to herself that as soon as she grew up, she would have a four-legged friend of her own.

As the years passed, Jacqui never forgot her resolution that she would one day have her own dog. But finding the right time was harder than she expected. She knew of people who had dogs when they really shouldn't – people who left them at home all day while they went to work, or kept them in a flat that was too small or that didn't have a proper outdoor space for a dog to play in. Jacqui wanted her pet to have the happiest life possible, which meant waiting until she could give it all the time and space it would need. And although she had lots of love to lavish on a dog, she would need to think about the money it would cost too.

So, for a while, Jacqui focused on other grown-up things. She got a job she enjoyed, and worked hard at her career. She fell in love with a man called Chris and they got married. Life as an adult was good, but in the back of her mind Jacqui felt that the one thing missing in her life was the dog she had always longed for.

Then, at last, the time came.

Between them, Jacqui and Chris decided that Jacqui could cut down to working part-time. They had a lovely big house in the country and Jacqui thought of all the extra days she would now have to spend in it. Then she thought all that spare time would be made delightfully, wondrously, magnificently better with … a dog!

Jacqui wanted to rehome a rescue dog instead of buying a puppy from a breeder or pet shop, so she went to Dogs Trust Newbury to look for her perfect and long-awaited dog. Even though the rehoming centre was a happy, bustling place and the residents were loved and well cared for, it was heartbreaking to think every one of the dogs there needed a home. Jacqui wished she could take them all home with her, but knew she could only choose one.

She visited the rehoming centre every week, greeting all the residents and trying to make the difficult decision of whom to adopt.

And then one day she saw him.

Whipping his long black tail back and forth, grinning, and blinking at her from inside his kennel, was five-year-old crossbreed Morris.

'He was so smiley and happy – as soon as I saw him I knew he was the one,' says Jacqui, matter-of-factly. 'I just couldn't walk past him. Somehow, without even having to think about it, I had decided.'

Morris was a little black collie-cross who had

been found straying in Wales and was brought to Dogs Trust Bridgend, then moved to Newbury. For many stray dogs, the experience of being abandoned and having to survive on their own leaves them very troubled. There was evidence that Morris had once broken one of his legs and the vet thought it was possible that he had been beaten by his previous owners. But even those horrible experiences could not break Morris's happy, loving character.

'Somehow I knew as soon as I set eyes on him that I would be taking Morris home, but I was even more certain when I took him out for a test walk,' says Jacqui. 'He smiled and smiled the whole time. We were instantly friends and had a wonderful time together on that walk. I didn't think I had ever met a lovelier dog.'

Jacqui told the rehoming centre staff that she wanted to give Morris a home, and a few days later, while all the checks and paperwork were being done, she brought her husband Chris to meet him too. Chris agreed the happy dog was irresistible and so, after only a short stay at Dogs Trust Newbury, Morris had found his forever home. It was January – a new year and a new start for Morris.

'Morris was just so laid back and friendly that he was spotted and snapped up in no time,' says assistant manager Jenny. 'He was playful and affectionate with people and other dogs, so we knew he would settle into a new home easily.'

And never did a dog settle into a new home more easily than Morris. 'The first day we took him home, he jumped out of the car and walked straight up the path and into the house,' Jacqui says. 'Completely unprompted, he trotted into the kitchen, and sat down on his bed, as if he'd always lived there. It was fantastic – Morris and I looked at each other and it was as if we both knew we were meant for each other.

'The one time Morris has ever messed in the house was on that first night, because he was a little confused I suppose. But he was very upset about it, because he is naturally such a clean dog. And after that he settled into his new routine beautifully.'

Jacqui could tell Morris's past had been tough. 'He was definitely beaten before,' she says. 'We noticed that, even though he was a very happy dog, if a noise or sudden movement made him jump, or if someone raised their arm, Morris would cower in fear. It was absolutely heartbreaking, but we could only be pleased that he was with us now. We would make sure we showered him with all the love he deserved but didn't get in his old life.'

Morris adored Jacqui and Chris, and followed them happily wherever they went. And in no time at all, he struck up a wonderful friendship with the family cat, Jagger. The two of them played together in their big garden, which also had ducks and chickens, and even its own stream running through it. As the weather got warmer, Morris loved to bound about in the stream, and then to lie down on the grass and dry out in the sunshine.

And so the family spent those blissful summer months together. Morris was so much part of the family that Jacqui couldn't quite remember all those years she had spent without him, longing for a dog of her own.

But that carefree happiness was not to last, and in October, a terrible tragedy struck the family.

Both Morris and Jagger were diagnosed with a very serious disease – a type of cancer called lymphoma. Lymphoma is not contagious, so it was just a terrible coincidence that both Morris and Jagger got it at the same time.

'That October was an awful month for us,' says Jacqui. 'Sadly, we lost our beautiful cat to the illness. We had a great vet, who did everything he could to save her, but within two weeks Jagger died. Morris, who was suffering with the disease himself, missed her as much as we did.'

Even though the vet had never known a dog to

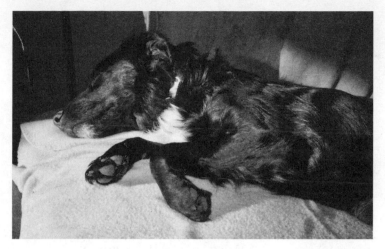

survive lymphoma before, he operated on Morris to try to stop the cancer. He took out a big lump the size of a golf ball from the dog's neck. He then put Morris on chemotherapy, which is a treatment that can sometimes cure cancer, but makes the patient feel tired and unwell.

'The cancer and the chemotherapy made Morris feel very sick indeed, and the vet told us that he would almost certainly die within the month,' says Jacqui. 'It was a very difficult time for all of us, but we tried to be brave and take one day at a time. So Morris struggled on, and against the odds he kept going beyond that month. He has a very strong will to live, my little chap.

'Everyone at the vet's thought Morris was remarkable. One of the nurses told us to go to the Animal Health Trust in Cambridgeshire, so we took Morris there to be examined. They did some serious tests on him – like taking samples of his liver and his other organs – but he was beautifully behaved. Even though I felt awful doing all these terrible things to him, he seemed to understand we were doing them because we loved him and were trying to help.'

So Jacqui and Chris took Morris to the Animal Health Trust every two months for more tests and treatments. And then, after a year, the vets had some astonishing news. They said they had never seen it happen before, but Morris seemed to have recovered from lymphoma!

'It was amazing,' says Jacqui. 'The vets said the only way they could possibly have cured the illness was if it was first treated in what's called

Stage One, and it's extremely rare for that to happen. Most owners only notice there's something wrong with their dog in stage two, and by that time it is too late to save them. But it looked like our Morris was that one-in-a-million dog whose lymphoma was caught and treated in stage one. We couldn't believe how lucky we were.'

Throughout that worrying year, Jacqui made a decision that if the impossible happened and Morris recovered from cancer, she would qualify him as a Pets As Therapy – or PAT – dog.

'I just thought Morris was so special, and he'd brought so much love and happiness to my life, that I should share him with other people,' she says. 'And because I had wanted a dog for all that time when I was younger, I wanted to share Morris with people who, for one reason or another, couldn't have a dog of their own.

'Lots of dog and cat lovers live in nursing homes, hospitals and hospices, where they aren't allowed to keep pets. So Pets As Therapy is an organisation that arranges for dogs and cats to visit those people regularly. They also visit different types of schools, day care centres and people who are suffering from various illnesses. The pets get lots of fuss and attention, and the people they visit get a little bit of that special joy that only animals can bring.'

So when Morris got the all-clear from the Animal Health Trust, after the huge celebrations and treats and cuddles all round, Jacqui got down to business. She contacted Pets As Therapy and put in an application for Morris to become a PAT dog.

'Any dog can become a PAT dog as long as they have been with their owner for over six months and are at least nine months old,' says Jacqui. 'They can be any breed or size but they do have to pass a test to prove they have a calm, friendly temperament. They have to show they're not snappy or nervous. Someone tests their reactions by dropping things out of sight, making different noises and so on, to make sure they are the right dog for the job.'

Despite Morris's dark and scary past, he passed the temperament test with no problems at all and, before he and his owner knew it, they were qualified as PAT volunteers. They started visiting a nearby nursing home once a week, and quickly Morris became a favourite visitor for a lot of people who lived there.

'Morris adored those visits too,' says Jacqui. 'He always got really excited when his special yellow PAT coat came out of the cupboard. I mean really excited – he would leap about and chase his tail round and round and round. When he had calmed down enough for me to put his coat on, I clipped a PAT lead to his collar, put on my own PAT T-shirt, and off we went.

'Then, suddenly, when we arrived at the nursing home and got out of the car, Morris always snapped into what I called his "calm mode". He would walk, stop, and sit exactly as I asked him.'

Poppy the Dogs Trust Dog

When they went inside, lots of the residents would be waiting in the lounge to see Morris, and so Jacqui would take him to greet each person in turn. The cheerful chap stood patiently, wagging his tail, while the residents stroked his thick black fur and chatted to him. After he had seen everyone in the lounge, Jacqui would take Morris from room to room, greeting people who couldn't leave their beds or who wanted one-on-one time with him.

'Some of the people were in wheelchairs or had trouble moving their hands, and for them I would have to push Morris a little closer so they could touch him. But he didn't mind one bit – he was very understanding and lapped up all the attention with glee. He struck up some wonderful friendships there.

'There was one lady in particular who I will never forget, she was called Mary. She loved dogs and kept them all her life, but as she became older and she found she couldn't look after herself, she had to move to the nursing home. Since Mary had to give up her own pets, she adored Morris's visits. She told me that seeing him was the highlight of her week, and whenever they met, he had a big smile on his face too.

'One day, Mary became very sick and I took Morris to see her in her bed. I lifted him up and put him on the bed so that her hand was touching him. And he lay there, perfectly still, for many quiet minutes while Mary gently touched his fur.

'The next day, Mary died. The last thing she said to me was how lovely it was that Morris had been to see her and, through the sadness, I felt proud that we had given her that special pleasure in her last hours of life. It's so nice to be able to do that for someone.'

So Morris continued his voluntary work for a long time, with his boundless enthusiasm, kindness and patience, when one day at home a big newspaper headline caught Jacqui's eye. Over her cup of coffee she read, 'Dogs Trust opens nominations for the first ever Dogs Trust

Weasel with new owner Carolyn

The photo shoot that made Weasel a star

Morris working as a PAT dog

© Nick Ridley Photography

Jess wows the crowd on an Agility course

Doctor Morris – Therapist Dog

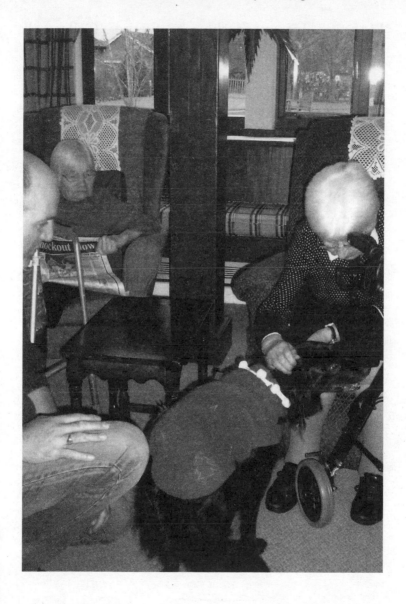

Honours.' Interested, she read further. 'Calling all proud dog owners across the UK!' the article continued. 'Do you own a gutsy greyhound, a talented terrier or a courageous crossbreed? Now is your chance to give your outstanding hound the recognition he or she deserves, as the UK's largest dog welfare charity calls for entries for the first ever Dogs Trust Honours awards.'

Amongst the categories was one that jumped straight out at Jacqui – the 'triumph over adversity' award.

Jacqui looked up from her paper, and then down at Morris, who was relaxing by her feet. He looked back at her and thumped his tail on the floor cheerfully. If ever there was an outstanding hound who had made it through the hard times, Morris was surely it. He hadn't just been abused and abandoned, and survived life as a stray; he'd recovered from a deadly disease, and now spent lots of his time bringing happiness to the elderly. He had done all these things with a smile on his face and a big wag in his tail. Jacqui felt a surge of pride for her wonderful dog and decided there and then to enter him for the award. She got the entry form, filled it in and sent it off.

A few weeks later, Jacqui received a letter through the post from Dogs Trust. Morris had been picked to go on the shortlist! That would mean the two of them would be travelling to London to go to the special awards ceremony.

As the days flew by and the ceremony came closer, Jacqui had come to terms with the fact that, as wonderful as Morris was, he probably wouldn't win the award. The most amazing dogs in the country had been nominated, and there could only be one winner. But it was wonderful to be shortlisted and it would be fantastic to attend the ceremony.

Finally, the day of the Honours arrived. Morris had been groomed and his soft black fur looked splendidly shiny. Jacqui wore a long black velvet dress, and the two of them travelled together to

London for the long-awaited evening.

'Well, what an experience it was!' remembers Jacqui. 'When we got there, everything looked so beautiful. There was champagne, chandeliers and celebrities everywhere, and lots of people in evening dress, and dogs too. Morris wore his usual big smile and wagged his tail non-stop.'

After chatting to lots of different people, Jacqui and Morris were shown to their seats, the lights dimmed and the ceremony began …

'It was marvellous hearing the stories of all those amazing dogs, but about halfway through, Morris started to get a bit overwhelmed by all the clapping,' Jacqui says. 'So we slipped out to have some quiet time. We had been out there less than five minutes when I heard the sound of a lady's heels running over the marble floor. She came towards us and she was saying something. After a moment or two I realised that she was saying that we had to go back in because Morris had won! He had won the triumph over adversity award!

'We quickly went back into the hall where everyone turned to look at us. Morris didn't mind the clapping this time! He knew something special was going on. We walked through all the tables and up on to the stage where we were presented with the award.

'I have never felt so proud of Morris. After hearing all the stories of dogs who overcome terrible difficulties, to think that the judges thought that Morris deserved the award was amazing. I was so overwhelmed, I can't even remember what I said in the acceptance speech.'

So Morris was honoured that evening for everything he had been through and all that he had given back to his community as a PAT dog.

But now he has got older, Morris has had some more difficulties with his health. 'Since he won the triumph over adversity award, we've been told poor Morris has a problem with his nerves in his back legs and his tail,' says Jacqui, sadly. 'He finds it hard to stand and sit like he used to, and he isn't

able to lift his tail as high as he once could to wag it. And the vets say the illness will get worse.'

So Morris has retired as a PAT dog because that involves lots of moving about into different positions, which he just can't do anymore. But his treatment is working well. He still goes for a walk every day, although it's a lot slower and not so far as before. And even though he is older now and his eyesight and hearing have got worse, his love of life has not faded one bit.

'Morris is a fabulous little dog,' says Jacqui, glowing with pride as she looks at the four-legged friend she always wanted. 'He has bounced back from everything life has chucked at him, which has been a lot. And he did so much for elderly people as a PAT dog, we think it's his turn to be spoilt rotten.

'After everything he has been through, everything he has done, and for everything he is, we love Morris to pieces. Award or no award, he is honoured in our house every single day.'

Jess Steals the Show

Wag, wag! Hello, it's Poppy.

I sometimes think life is like a doggy Agility course. We have to leap over obstacles and weave our way through problems. We must balance carefully so we don't fall, and sometimes we can't even see where we're heading, like we're crawling through a tunnel. But if we do all these things as best we can, with a spring in our step and a wag in our tail, we'll get big rewards, and have tremendous fun along the way.

So who better to show you how full of life we dogs can be than a professional Agility dog? Meet Jess: sporty on the outside, scatty on the inside, with a wicked sense of humour but a heart as golden as her fur.

Licks and more licks,

Pops xxx

As soon as she sets off around the rescue dog Agility course, it is plain to see that Jess was born to perform. Silence falls as chattering folk stop what they are saying mid-sentence and, squinting against the bright July sun, they gaze into the ring in amazement. Ice creams drip down their cones as people forget to lick them and a lost balloon floats up quietly into the sky. Everyone in the audience is captivated by the golden dog flashing expertly around the ring.

Led by her owner, Helen, Jess belts up and down A-frames at amazing speeds. She zooms through tunnels like a bullet and springs over jumps and hurdles effortlessly. Her eyes shine and her golden fur glistens in the sunlight.

She is breathtaking to watch.

Just as the crowd are thinking that they must be witnessing a top professional in action, suddenly, out of the blue, Jess stops. But she is only halfway through the course. The nimble dog stands completely still at the entrance to a tunnel and wags her tail naughtily. A chuckle is released from the crowd, and people mutter to each other *What's going on? What on earth is she doing?* Helen is sweeping her arm frantically towards the tunnel, trying to get her dog to go through. With her pink tongue hanging out and her mouth pulled into a big smile, Jess looks at Helen, then at the tunnel. She looks to the crowd, and then back at the tunnel. And suddenly she is on the move again. But she doesn't crawl through the tunnel like she's supposed to. Instead, the cheeky dog springs on to the top of it! The chuckles in the crowd erupt into full laughter and clapping as Jess swaggers along the roof of the tunnel, swinging her tail and clearly enjoying her surprise performance.

'She only does it to embarrass me,' says Helen. 'I've even been told off by other handlers who say their dogs never showed that sort of cheeky behaviour in the ring until they met Jess, and now they're skipping along the tops of tunnels too!'

Once she gets to the end of the tunnel and jumps down on to the grass, Jess is back in professional mode. Silence descends over the crowd once again as the agile dog gets back up to full speed, obeying Helen's every direction. She takes more jumps, A-frames and tunnels with ease. She moves with such grace and elegance that the audience is awed. And then she comes to the weave.

'Jess just *cannot* be bothered with the weave,' says Helen. 'It's too boring for her. She'd rather bolt off and do a few jumps instead and come back when I've given up trying to make her do it!'

Well, seeing Jess refuse to weave in and out of

the poles, and instead run off to give her own unique display sends the audience wild. The delighted squeals, laughter and clapping are even louder than before as the dog heads back the way she came, leaping over jumps she's already done, darting through a few tunnels and finally hurtling back to her owner. Helen ruffles Jess's fur in good-natured exasperation and the two of them finish the course together. They leave the ring to deafening cheering and applause, and for the rest of the afternoon everyone is talking about what a spectacle Jess's performance was.

It's just as well the Dogs Trust rescue dog Agility team is not competitive. 'The team was set up to show the public how rescue dogs can be far more than just dogs who need homes,' says Jack, the team's manager. 'We want to show how varied dogs can be, and how much fun people can have with them. We've got all shapes and sizes of dog, speedy ones and more laid-back ones. We've got pedigree dogs and crossbreeds, and the handlers are all ages. We've got dogs who are Agility champions, some who are novices, and some, like Jess, who are wonderful show-offs in the ring. When it comes to a great performance, Jess has never let me down. Everybody remembers her, and that's what our team is all about.'

It was midsummer when Helen first met and fell in love with her superstar Jess. 'I was at Dogs Trust Kenilworth looking for my first dog,' she says. 'I had dogs when I was little but never one of my very own, so I was really excited. I was looking for a sparky, energetic dog and, as I was walking through the kennels, there was one little lady who was almost bursting with joy. She had the build of a small lurcher but the colouring of a yellow labrador, with lovely, soft, blonde fur. She pushed herself up against the window of the kennel as I approached, as if she was trying to lean against me through the glass. Her ears were pressed flat against her head and she looked at me with big, round, brown eyes. I crouched down to say hello to her, her tail started wagging, and from then on it didn't stop!'

Helen had wanted to do Agility training before she had even met Jess. 'Working in partnership like that looked like so much fun for the dog and the handler too,' she says. 'I love being out and about and active, so I was really keen on trying Agility, as well as looking for a doggy companion to come on long walks in the countryside.

'Jess was so lovely and enthusiastic I had to find out more about her. I was allowed to take her out for a walk next to the rehoming centre, so we could get to know each other a bit. And as soon as we got outside, tail still wagging, she tried to drag me to the exercise area. She had so much energy about her, and was really bright too. I brought my partner Dave to meet her and together we decided that she was definitely the one for us.

'I remember sitting in reception with Jess the day we got her, waiting to fill in the final rehoming form. She was sitting next to us, whining and whining non-stop with excitement at everything that was going on around her. Dave and I looked at each other and wondered for a moment if we'd bitten off more than we could chew with this dog. But Jess's excitement was so infectious, we just grinned at each other and signed the papers happily.'

Helen and Dave couldn't wait to take Jess home. And, as they suspected, she made a wonderful, if excitable, new member of the family. When she was out on her walks, she loved to chase anything and everything, but she settled happily into life at Helen and Dave's with no problems at all.

Well, there was one, small problem …

Helen was a teacher in a school so, in the morning, she would take Jess out for a long run, dish up a hearty breakfast for her, and off she would go to her morning lessons. At lunchtime, Helen would come back to have some lunch and spend some time with Jess, who jumped around with joy when she saw her owner and showered her with love. She let the bouncy dog have a run around in the garden and played games with her until she had to go back to school for the afternoon.

'When I came home at the end of the day, Jess would bound up to meet me at the door again, full of licks and affection – like butter wouldn't melt! But quickly I would discover that something of mine was missing from its usual place,' says Helen. 'Sometimes I couldn't find a shoe, sometimes my fleece would have vanished from the hook, all sorts of things disappeared.'

But it didn't matter what it was, Helen always knew where she could find it – in Jess's bed. 'She would steal anything she could get her thieving little paws on!' Helen says. 'It was like she was trying to tell me that she did not approve of me going out again after lunch – even though it was only for a couple of hours. When I went to her bed to find what she'd taken, there it would be, in the folds of her blanket and a little bit soggy and nibbled.'

Helen tried to break Jess's habit by removing anything the cheeky dog could get hold of – packing everything into drawers and cupboards out of Jess's reach. Eventually, the plan worked and Helen could leave her things around the house again without fear of Jess stealing them.

The school holidays came and Jess and Helen would spend their days either playing games in the garden at home, or going for long walks. 'We had a lovely time together in the holidays,' says Helen. 'If we went to woodland, Jess would make herself busy diving in and out of bushes or with her nose to the ground and her tail on a permanent wag setting. And if we went anywhere with a big open space, she would always nag me for a game of something, so I had to make sure I always brought a ball for her. She was really fantastic company – so funny and full of beans.'

But when the holidays ended and Helen had to go back to school, sure enough, Jess's stealing habit started all over again. 'I think it's because she got so used to spending all her time with me,' says Helen. 'Even though I didn't work very long days, and always came back to see her at lunchtime, it was like Jess wanted to give me a little slap on the wrists. Seeing her curled up in her bed with a stolen item was really funny though – she always had the stupidest expression on her face and her tail would almost be wagging off her body! She clearly knew she'd done something wrong, but looking at her funny, guilty little face, it was impossible to be cross with her. She's just really cheeky, which I love about her.'

And Jess did not just steal clothes and shoes. She took all sorts of weird and wonderful things. 'I think Jess's most impressive steal ever was half a rhubarb crumble, which she managed to get off the kitchen counter, across the kitchen, through the hall and into her bed. After searching in the fridge, the oven and everywhere you would expect a rhubarb crumble to be, I thought I was going mad. Later that day of course, there it was in Jess's bed. Amazingly, it was completely intact! She didn't want to eat it, she just wanted to steal it.

'I decided to use her love of transporting things around the house to my advantage, and we had all sorts of fun. Jess liked to snatch the post from the letterbox, so Dave and I trained her to bring it up to us if we were having a lie-in at the weekend. She loved doing that, and we got our letters delivered straight to our hands, which was brilliant, even though there were a few teeth marks in them.'

So, even though Jess had some funny little habits, she was clearly a very clever dog and Helen knew she would be great to train. They started off with some obedience training, which Jess was excellent at. Helen says, 'Because she adored chasing things, and wasn't very good at coming back when asked, I thought obedience training would help her. And it would be something fun that we could do together before we tried Agility.'

So every week, Helen and her golden dog went off to obedience training. And just as Helen thought, Jess was a natural. In no time at all, she learned how to sit, come, wait and lie down. She loved learning new things and pleasing her owner, and she especially loved the little treats she got as a reward for getting things right. 'Whenever Jess learned a new set of commands, we had to take a test,' says Helen. 'Jess sailed through every one, and each time we were put up into a more advanced class until we reached the top.

'I remember the last, most difficult test of all. It was called *stop the dog*,' says Helen. 'I was really nervous because it focused on the handler's ability to stop their dog from ten paces away. It's an important skill to have in an emergency – for example if your dog has crossed a busy road and you don't want them to cross again to get back to you. That sort of test is especially hard for Jess –

because she loves either chasing things or being right by my side.'

So, before the final test, Helen and Jess were out in all weathers, practising hard. And in the end their hard work paid off, because when the test came, they performed a faultless *stop the dog*. Jess got lots of treats that afternoon.

Now that they had come to the end of their obedience training and had developed a great bond from working together, Helen thought it was time to try Agility. She found a local training group and off they went.

'Obviously, at first, Jess didn't have a clue what she was supposed to do with all that equipment,' says Helen. 'But our obedience training really helped me to guide her, and she picked up all the different obstacles really quickly. Well, apart from the weave of course. She knew what to do, but she decided very early on that she didn't fancy doing it! It was nice for her to be able to show off a bit though, and put her amazing speed to use too. I always say that Jess doesn't do anything at half-speed – it's either a hundred miles an hour or stop!'

One day at their Agility class, as Jess was bounding over hurdles, eyes wide and tail aloft with joy, and Helen was giving her lots of words of encouragement, a lady came up to them who recognised Jess. The lady happened to work at Dogs Trust Kenilworth, and had helped look after Jess when she was first brought in after being found straying in Solihull. 'She told me she knew Jess as soon as she saw her distinctive blonde fluff and the pale stripe down her nose,' says Helen. 'And when she saw her running, she was certain it was Jess.'

Jess recognised the lady too, and greeted her by leaning her golden body up against her legs, looking up and wagging her tail. The lady ruffled the dog's silky fur and commented on how well and happy she looked. She told Helen about the Dogs Trust rescue dog Agility team, and said Jess

should definitely join. Dogs from the five biggest dog rescue charities – Battersea Dogs Home, The Blue Cross, Dogs Trust, RSPCA and Wood Green Animal Shelters – could be members. And because the team was set up for demonstrations rather than competitions, Jack, the manager, was looking for great performances and sparkling personalities. It was clear to see that Jess had both.

'Even though I do take her to some competitions now, we are never going to be the best competitive dog and handler and we don't take it too seriously,' says Helen. 'Going round the ring absolutely perfectly is just not Jess's style, because she loves adding her own special touches. She's never won anything yet – she's just too cheeky. So I thought the rescue dog Agility team would be perfect, because cheekiness was just what Jack wanted.'

Jack absolutely agrees. 'One of the best spur-of-the-moment performances a member of the rescue dog Agility team has given was from a fantastic black German shepherd,' he says. 'He soared over the hurdles and was just about to take the A-frame, but instead jumped straight over the fence and into the crowd. With everyone watching, he trotted up the steps, along one of the rows of seats, and sat down in front of a lady who was eating a sandwich. Of course, by now everyone was laughing, including the lady with the sandwich. She tore him off a bit, which he chewed and swallowed and then calmly walked back along the row of seats, back down the steps, over the fence and carried on with what he'd been doing in the ring. Dogs like that are brilliant for our team – showing that they're not robots and they're good at having lots of fun.'

Well it would be hard to find a dog less robotic than Jess, and she certainly has huge amounts of fun in her life. Now, instead of stealing from her owner, she mostly brings things to her. 'She'll bring me all sorts of things these days,' Helen says. 'She's such a clown. She loves bringing me my phone and drops other random things into my lap all the time too. If she knows there are treats in my bag, she'll bring the bag to me and poke it with her nose asking me to give her one. If I don't, she'll manage to unzip it and help herself.

'Last Christmas Dave and I were playing a game with about fourteen members of my family that involved betting with fake money. Dave and I were terrible at the game and lost all our money really quickly. But Jess was there and she fancied a bit of attention, so she kept stealing the paper money from the other players and bringing it to us!'

But Jess is most definitely a crook with a heart. 'She is such a softie, it's unbelievable,' Helen says. 'And because of the joys of owning Jess, we now own a grand total of seven dogs. As well as our cheeky blonde beauty, there's Hullabaloo, Dot, Kai, Paddy, Tara and the latest addition is Widget. Jess is like the mummy dog — she's just so lovely to everyone. All the others have really taken to her, especially the puppies. She plays with them and teaches them things. She even lets them climb all over her and chew her neck.'

But even though Jess is the second oldest dog in the home, when the toys come out, her 'mummy dog' duties are brushed aside and she is always the first one there. 'She's very fast and determined, so often she'll win the race for the toy fair and square,' says Helen. 'But if it looks like she's losing, she doesn't mind cheating and barging others out of the way. The other dogs don't mind though. They are all quite happy to let Jess win every time in any chasing game, because they love her so much and are grateful for all the fun she brings to their lives.

'And I feel exactly the same way. That's why, when she shows me up at competitions, nags me all the time for games and treats, and I find rhubarb crumbles and mobile phones in her bed, I have to smile and love her even more.'

The Oakfield Oldies

Wags to you, readers!

Now, as everybody knows, when you're in need of a race, a chase or just a good romp around in the garden, there's no better playmate than a dog. If you're bored with all the games you know, just ask a dog and we can easily come up with a new one. We don't need expensive toys or the latest computer games to show you a good time! With bags of energy, our four legs, and a big open space, we can create the best games ever.

But you must remember – just like people, we do not stay young for ever. And just like people, when we get older we start to slow down a bit. Our fur can go a bit grey around our beards, our bones can start to creak, and we often find it difficult to bounce about like we used to.

As we get older, we dogs often get lots of the same health problems that elderly humans get. Diseases like diabetes or arthritis may start to set in. Just like people, our eyesight can get hazy and we can go a bit deaf. We may even go slightly dotty and forget where we are!

However, one thing that never changes is that we are always your best friend. With lots of love and care from our owners, we can still give and receive as much happiness as when we're young.

Elderly dogs may prefer gentle strolls or a snooze by the fire to their old running races, but they still adore spending time with their owners out in the fresh air or just at home. And even if they lose interest in chasing their tail or leaping a metre into the air to catch a speeding frisbee, they never lose their sense of fun. And, most importantly, dogs never run out of love no matter how old they get.

It's very sad, but old dogs can also find themselves homeless. Some owners abandon their oldies because they find them difficult or tiresome to look after. Sometimes old dogs also have elderly owners who pass away before them. So when their owner dies, the poor dog is left with no owner and no home either.

That's why Dogs Trust decided to open Oakfield, the Old Dogs' Home dedicated to looking after our more elderly canine residents in a happy home environment. Please enjoy this touching tale, but a word of warning – you should keep a tissue handy!

All my licks,
Poppy xxx

Ten years ago, everything was ticking along as normal at Dogs Trust Roden. The kennels were bustling with dogs playing with their kennel-mates and greeting passers-by with wags and woofs. Reception was busy looking after people who were bringing dogs in or taking them home. The vet was in his surgery prescribing medicine and planning operations for sick dogs. Doggy behaviour training was going on in one of the exercise areas, and on the big fields next to the rehoming centre lots of dogs were enjoying a walk in the fresh air with their canine carers.

One of the dogs out on the fields that day was

Wilfred, a gorgeous doberman-cross whose owner had died so he had come to Dogs Trust to find a new one. Being a doddery fifteen-year-old, Wilfred was struggling to keep up with the young bounders who were hurtling about and rolling around boisterously on the grass. Even though fifteen is still very young for humans, in dog years it is quite elderly, so Wilfred preferred to move his creaky black body slowly. On his spindly legs, he would tiptoe carefully around obstacles instead of barging straight through them like the younger fellows.

The difference in ages between the dogs made keeping them all together on the field a difficult task for the canine carer Paul. When he rushed ahead to keep up with the younger dogs, poor Wilfred was left miles behind, and when he slowed down to Wilfred's pace, the other dogs became little bouncing specks ahead of him.

Paul thought how wonderful it would be if Wilfred could live somewhere he didn't have to keep up with the younger ones – somewhere he could just relax, be himself and take life at his own pace until that special new owner came along. At a rickety fifteen years old and having just lost his owner, lovely Wilfred deserved to enjoy his life.

Sadly, it can be difficult to rehome old dogs. If they have health problems, they take more effort to look after, and lots of people look for energetic younger dogs to take into their families. Paul was pondering this and crossing his fingers that Wilfred would find a happy new home soon, when he spotted a sign that said 'For Sale' on the opposite side of the field. He wandered slowly over to investigate with old Wilfred tottering beside him, while the other three dogs did forward rolls over each other in a game they had made up on the spot.

Standing next to the sign, Paul and Wilfred peered through the bushes and saw a big, beautiful house with a gravel driveway that looked like it would satisfyingly *crunch* when you walked on it.

The house was very impressive and built of red brick. It was two floors high, with four large, curved windows at the front. The word 'Oakfield' was carved into a big polished piece of wood mounted next to the door. Paul stared at the house for ages, thinking how funny it was that he had just been imagining Wilfred's perfect new home, and it looked exactly like that!

All four of the dogs headed back to the kennels, Paul trying hard to keep them all together. When he got back, he mentioned the empty 'Oakfield' house to Louise, the manager. He told her how he wished Wilfred could live in a house like that. With a smile, Louise agreed that would be wonderful for Wilfred and other old dogs like him. They talked about the possibilities for a long time and then Louise picked up the phone to Dogs Trust HQ in London. And so the discussions started ...

Some Dogs Trust staff went to see what Oakfield looked like inside, to make sure it would be suitable for lots of doddery four-legged dears. Soon after, everybody around the country who worked for Dogs Trust was talking about the new 'old dogs' home' that the charity was opening. Everyone agreed it was an amazing idea, but what would it look like? How many dogs would live there? Would Dogs Trust staff live there too? There would be so much to sort out.

'As soon as I heard about the plans for Oakfield, and people began to talk about who would be living there, my mind started racing,' says Kerrie, who had been working at Dogs Trust Roden for three years. 'I had heard of people living at retirement homes before, but not doggy retirement homes! Living with all those old dogs would involve a lot of work, but I couldn't stop thinking about how much I would love it.

'Lots of the oldies I had worked with during my time at Dogs Trust had found kennel life hard, and I really wanted to help dogs like them. Older dogs can find it difficult to adjust to kennels because they have lived in stable homes for so much of their lives. I wanted to be the person who could give them back that security and happiness.

'I already had three dogs of my own, but I felt certain they would enjoy living in an old dogs' home. One was quite old, and the other two were so sweet and gentle with him, I knew they would be very kind to other old dogs too.'

So when discussions about who would be living at Oakfield began, Kerrie eagerly volunteered. After a nail-biting wait, Louise told her that the job was hers. She was delighted! Sarah, who also worked at Dogs Trust Roden, was chosen to work with her – she had her own dog too. Kerrie and Sarah got straight to work packing up their things and getting ready to embark on their exciting new life at the old dogs' home.

One day in late August, the two girls finally moved in. Kerrie's dogs, Alki, Raid and Spot, made instant friends with Sarah's dog Barney, and all six housemates got along wonderfully.

Everyone was so excited to be living in the big house. John, the Dogs Trust Roden caretaker, had freshly painted every room so the whole place smelt fresh and new. He had also done some renovation to make it comfortable for Kerrie and Sarah and suitable for lots of old dogs to live there. He had put in special stair-gates, because the last thing any old dog needs is a bad fall down the stairs.

'The house was gorgeous,' says Kerrie. 'There were two huge living-rooms downstairs, where we'd put lots of comfy sofas and dog beds. Alki, Raid, Spot and Barney were delighted with all the cosy furniture, but we couldn't wait for more doggy residents to be curled up on it with them.

'Upstairs, Sarah and I had nice big bedrooms to move all our own things into. Everything was just perfect. We knew our new life would involve lots of work, but we were really looking forward to getting started.'

The two went shopping together for pictures, flowers and other bits and pieces to make their home bright and jolly. Then, in just two weeks, their first elderly doggy housemate moved in. Old doberman-cross Wilfred had already been rehomed, so Dogs Trust had to choose another dog to be the first Oakfield resident.

'Laddie was gorgeous!' says Kerrie. 'He was a little twelve-year-old whippet, and he settled in straight away. He had some arthritis in his joints, but apart from that he was completely healthy. He'd been very nervous and shy in kennels but he came out of his shell when he moved in with us. Oakfield was a success straight away, because within a couple of weeks Laddie was rehomed.

'It was wonderful because both of us were secretly thinking that he might be living with us for the rest of his life. But we were wrong! Because he was so happy to be living in a real home, he totally relaxed and his natural outgoing character shone through.

'One day we took him down to the rehoming centre to meet a couple who were interested in an older dog. In just a few minutes they fell in love with him and couldn't resist.

'Of course it was fantastic, but Sarah and I couldn't help feeling sad because we had got so used to having lovely Laddie at home with us. He was such a pleasure to live with. Even though we got attached to other dogs we knew at the rehoming centre, it felt different seeing Laddie go to a new home. He had watched TV with us in the evenings and curled up on our laps when he was sleepy. The other dogs missed him too and sulked for a bit.

'We knew life at Oakfield would involve some sadness as well as happiness, so we had to be prepared for that.'

So Laddie moved to his new home, but before they knew it, Kerrie and Sarah were living with fourteen dogs! One of Kerrie's dogs was old too, so that meant they were sharing their home with eleven oldies.

The old dogs love to take life easy and sleep a lot, so there are always furry bodies curled up on all the soft squishy surfaces in the living rooms.

'In the evenings, just getting to the kitchen is like an obstacle course and can take quite a long time,' says Kerrie, laughing. 'And the sounds of all those old dogs snoring away on their cushions and beds can get noisy too!

'There are lots of funny and endearing things about living with all those old dogs. Whenever one of us is cooking in the kitchen, there is a row of faces staring at us – like a doggy audience!

'And often, if one of us heads to the sofa, one of the oldies slyly gets there before us, even though there are dog beds everywhere. They all agree on their favourite places to sleep amongst themselves, and lots of them enjoy a cuddle on the sofa with Sarah or me.

'Our own dogs are lovely to the oldies too. They act differently with the Oakfield residents depending on who they are. They play with the dogs who are young at heart, but are much gentler with the really doddery ones. It is touching to see how sensitively they treat the oldies.

'We quickly got used to looking after dogs with all sorts of illnesses. We have diabetic dogs, who must have a very strict diet and eat only at certain times, and dogs who suffer from epilepsy and have to take medicine several times a day. Walking fourteen dogs every day is quite a challenge too!'

But what the girls quickly noticed was that the old dogs take on a new lease of life when they move to Oakfield. They seem to get younger and their characters begin to shine through again.

The old dogs' home is working wonderfully, and many of the oldies are being rehomed or fostered. Fostering is what happens when a Dogs Trust dog has a health problem that will mean lots of vet's fees. The dog is rehomed to the new owner, but Dogs Trust agrees to pay for the trips to the vet. The charity does this to make sure that people do not judge a dog by how much he or she will cost to look after. A dog who needs to take medicine can still have a great character and make a lovely addition to a family.

So, old dogs are being fostered to new owners regularly. 'We never take visitors into Oakfield, because it's the dogs' home and we want them to feel safe and secure,' says Kerrie. 'But we often take them for a walk down to the rehoming centre if we think somebody might be interested in rehoming or fostering them. People can also look at pictures of the oldies on the Dogs Trust website.' By living with them, the girls know so much about the old dogs that they can talk for ages about each one's character and all their funny little ways.

Of course, some of the oldies live the final days of their lives at Oakfield. 'It never gets any easier to cope when one of our dogs dies,' says Kerrie. 'It is heartbreaking every time, because we build such a bond with them. While they live here, they are our dogs, and we are their owners. They rely on us for everything they need and we come to love them dearly.

'But I'm glad that those dogs can enjoy the last days of their lives in a caring home, just as every dog deserves. I feel proud that I can offer them that, especially because we often don't know where they have come from or what sort of life they have had before.'

Two years after Oakfield opened, Sarah moved

out and a lady called Tracey moved in with her two dogs Hyo and Bonnie. All three of them were delighted to be living in the unusual house with all the doggy housemates, and settled into Oakfield life quickly.

During the years that followed, the girls grew so fond of some of their residents that they decided to foster them themselves. That way Kerrie and Tracey knew for sure those dogs would be spending their last days with them in the happy comfort of Oakfield.

Tracey fostered a lab-cross called Oscar, Emmy the shih tzu, and Pru who was a yorkie-cross. Kerry fostered two Jack Russells called Biddy and Ursula, Cherry the yorkie, and a fluffy pekinese called Flea. 'Flea was a hilarious old thing!' says Kerrie. 'She would manage to make her way up into the kitchen cupboards, and sit inside making little gurgling noises until I went to find her. She was always pleased when I discovered her and took her down. She would wag her tail good-

© Andy Catterall

akfield Old Dogs' Home gives
ADs a wonderful new home

© Andy Catterall

Education officer, Natalie, with Megan and Belle

Natalie and Megan
at work in a classroom
using a Nintendo to
teach schoolchildren
how to be good
dog owners

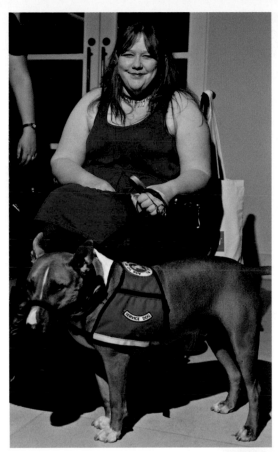

Arrow with his owner Wolfie

Arrow looking smart in the official assistance dog uniform he worked so hard to get

Dogs Trust
Ambassador
Mr Magoo

naturedly, but then a few minutes later she would creep off and do it again!

'In fact, I think I've seen every type of strange doggy behaviour in the ten years I've lived at Oakfield. We used to have one little dog who would jump on the windowsill as soon as the people left the house and stay there without moving at all until we came back. You could always see his little shadow through the curtain. We used to call him the neighbour-hood watch!'

Since the first day she moved in, Kerrie has lived with well over three hundred Oakfield oldies, and loves her job and her doggy housemates more than ever.

'At the moment Oakfield only has three residents who are looking for a home but we're waiting for some more to move in. There's Charlie, who's a seventeen-year-old Jack Russell, but who thinks he's only eight or nine. He's full of fun and follows Monty the lab around like his shadow. Monty is only six but he suffers from

epilepsy. He has a fit about every two weeks so he needs lots of looking after, and Oakfield is the perfect place for that. We also have twelve-year-old June, a rather overweight lab-cross who is on a diet! She doesn't like it very much, but she'll feel much happier and will be able to move around better when she's lost some weight.

'Most of the Oakfield oldies we have lived with over the years have gone to happy new homes. We're proud of that achievement. Before we opened the home we didn't think we would be rehoming dogs from Oakfield. However, I've also seen about forty of my dear doggy housemates pass away,' says Kerrie, 'which is very difficult indeed.

'We had some sad news yesterday that a lovely dog who, only recently fostered from Oakfield, has just passed away. She was a beautiful, fluffy German shepherd called Lady, and her new owners adored her as much as Tracey and I did. They told us that on her first night she went into their kitchen and raided every single cupboard and the fridge. They woke up in the morning and found she'd eaten half a sack of potatoes! She often did that sort of thing when she was living at Oakfield. But she was so gentle with such big shiny brown eyes, you just couldn't be cross with her – you could only laugh and ruffle her long fur. She only lived with her new family for a few short weeks, but I am certain she brought lots of laughter and happiness in that time and her owners felt very proud to have known her.

'There is so much happiness and heartbreak in

my job, and often the two feelings come at the same time. There's always a tear in my eye when one of the Oakfield oldies leaves for a new home, but it's a happy kind of sadness. I know they will be going to a caring owner who will look after them and show them all the love they deserve in their old age.

'The worst thing is when we lose a dog, but even then we feel glad that they spent their last days with more care and comfort than they could have wished for. They were the lucky ones – I wish every dog could have such a happy ending to their story.

'But despite all the hard work and tears, I feel like I am the luckiest of everyone. Having just one dog is joyful, but I have had the love, company and cuddles of over three hundred gorgeous dogs. I can't imagine a happier life than that!

'I know loads of people who would jump at the chance to swap places with me, but I wouldn't give up Oakfield life for anything!'

Megan goes to School

Hello readers, wag, wag!

Imagine you're having a horrible nightmare. You are by yourself in bed and suddenly, out of the darkness, a terrifying creature comes towards you. Its strange body is covered in long grey hair and is held up by four spindly legs. It has dark, flashing eyes and huge, pointy teeth. Terrified, you cling to the duvet, wishing it would go away. The beast looks you straight in the eye and swings its heavy, hairy tail back and forth. It unleashes a very long, very pink tongue from its scary mouth and licks its weird black nose. You scream in horror and wake up!

Now everybody has nightmares about scary monsters from time to time, but would you believe, readers, that some people see this terrifying creature every time they look at *me*?

Sometimes, people who haven't met a dog before think I want to use my big teeth to chew *them*! They don't realise I just want to be friends, and the only thing I'm interested in chomping on is my rubber chicken. When I wag my tail and hold up my paw, they don't see the offer of a polite handshake – they only see my big claws coming towards them.

Of course it's important that we are careful around anybody we don't know, both dogs and people, but those who are terrified of all dogs are missing out on all that we friends-on-four-legs have to offer. So, to teach children about the delights of dogs and how to be safe around them, Dogs Trust employs people and pooches to give classes in schools across the country.

Meet Megan – one half of a human-and-dog team who turns even the most terrified kids into devoted dog-lovers.

Licks,

Pops xxx

'I call it the Megan effect!' says Natalie. 'She's an expert in building people's confidence and making them trust her. Just yesterday I had three boys in my class who told me they were terrified of dogs. They were wary of Megan at first but by the end of the lesson they couldn't take their hands off her! She enjoyed them stroking her, too – but then again she never gets bored with admirers making a fuss of her.'

According to Dogs Trust education officer Natalie, Megan knows she has a talent for making people love dogs. That's why the little black Patterdale is always the first to bound down the stairs in the morning when Natalie calls for a doggy volunteer to come to school with her.

Natalie wears a smart Dogs Trust sweatshirt and clips a yellow Dogs Trust lead to Megan's collar, and together they hop in the car to drive to their first lesson of the day. 'We usually have between two and six workshops a day in different schools around London,' says Natalie. 'Megan and I stand at the front of the class. I do all the talking but of course everyone is staring at her! After all, it's not every day you see a dog in the classroom. I introduce us both and then, using Megan as my helper, I teach the children about all sorts of different doggy things.

'Sometimes we teach a class about what a dog needs to be healthy and happy – like proper food, exercise, company and a nice place to sleep. Other lessons are about how to be a responsible dog owner – like considering the cost of a dog before getting one, and whether you can give it the time, space and love it needs. We teach some lessons about the importance of microchipping and neutering, and we teach people how to be safe around dogs. All our lessons are specially designed to fit in with the school's teaching programme, and if the class has a special doggy interest we can focus on that too.

'For passionate dog-lovers in the class, sometimes I talk about the different careers they can have at Dogs Trust when they grow up. We have games and quizzes, and everyone gets to meet Megan personally and give her a stroke. By that time she has usually charmed the socks off everyone in the room, including the teachers.'

Being an education dog is a position of great responsibility because people often judge all dogs on their first doggy experience. One nip from the first dog you meet is enough to turn anyone into a cat person for life! But spend one hour with Megan and it seems you'll come out the biggest dog-lover ever.

'I've got three education dogs, and they're all

Patterdales,' says Natalie. 'I love Patterdales! There's Ealy, who's a big baby. He's in semi-retirement now, though, after years of hard service with me in schools. I've got Belle, who's adorable, but a bundle of excitement. And then there's Megan, who's just perfect. She's got such a lovely temperament. She's friendly to everybody, very easygoing and really responsive to people. She loves physical contact – pats and strokes and cuddles. And even if she's leaning her little body against someone's legs, or they're just touching her head, you can see she's happy. Even the most nervous person can't resist stroking a dog like that.'

But six-year-old Megan's journey to become a Dogs Trust education dog was not an easy one. A dog warden found the little dog wandering stray in Slough and took her to a local animal rescue centre. They didn't have room for her, so they had to turn the poor pooch away. The warden then brought her to Dogs Trust Harefield.

When Megan arrived at the centre, the staff

found the little stray delightful. She was so calm and happy, though she was covered in ticks. She would have picked up all those blood-sucking parasites out in the countryside, and whoever owned her before hadn't bothered to remove them from her skin. She also had some scars under her shiny black coat.

The staff thought little Megan could have been used for 'ratting', which is very dangerous for dogs. The dog is trained to chase after rats and kill them. Some people do this to control the number of rats on their land, but some also like to make dogs kill the little creatures for 'fun'. Of course, the terrified rats defend themselves and their babies using their long, sharp claws, but because they are much smaller, they almost always die. A lot of blood can be shed on both sides of the fight, and poor Megan was lucky she wasn't blinded.

The vet examined her, cleaned her up and sent her off, tail a-wagging, to a cosy warm kennel. It wouldn't be long before someone wanted to rehome a beautiful and outgoing dog like Megan.

And sure enough, within a few days, a young couple spotted her through the kennel window and were touched by her big brown eyes and sweet nature. They took her for a walk across the field and fell in love with her as she trotted cheerfully alongside them, as if she had always been part of the family.

Staff at the centre agreed that Megan would fit in beautifully with the couple, and that they could offer her the safe, happy home she deserved. So a week later, after all the proper checks had been made, Megan's future was settled. She trotted out of the centre to start her life with her new family.

Everyone was so happy for Megan, and for the couple, who had a brilliant new best friend in the little dog – until one day, a couple of months later, the phone rang at Dogs Trust Harefield. It was one of Megan's new owners, calling to say they wanted to bring her back to the centre! Shocked and baffled, the rehoming centre manager asked why.

Megan was uncontrollable off the lead, the lady told him, and although they loved her dearly, they couldn't cope with a dog who didn't come back when they called her.

The manager pleaded with them to keep Megan in her stable new home, because it would be so upsetting for her to feel abandoned all over again. He said that Dogs Trust would work with the three of them to train Megan how to behave better off the lead. Dogs Trust training staff are experts in understanding why dogs behave the way they do. Using the best and most up-to-date methods, they would give as much help as necessary to train Megan. She was such a good-natured dog that she would certainly want to please her owners – it would just be a matter of teaching her how.

But the owners were insistent. They couldn't cope and they weren't able to spare the time to train her, so, sadly, Megan was one of the very few rehomed dogs who are brought back to the centre. She was taken back to her kennel, where her kennel-mate was delighted to see her and joyfully bounded up to greet her. But Megan was clearly sad, and moped for a while, not understanding why she had left her home and family.

Before long, however, her cheerful spirit began to return and lots more people were stopping and crouching down next to her kennel to admire her.

Megan was approaching her destiny as an education dog, but she wasn't there yet.

'I remember the first time I saw Megan,' Natalie says, fondly. 'I was walking through reception at the rehoming centre on the way to my office to prepare the next day's lessons. Because I am usually out at schools, I don't always know all the dogs we have in the kennels. But I spotted a family in reception who were fussing over a little black Patterdale. Well, as you know, I'm a huge fan of Patterdales, but as they're quite a new breed, and northern, it's rare to see them around London. Of course, I had Ealy and Belle already, and I know lots about the breed so I went to chat to the family and the lovely, wriggly dog they were fussing over.

'They all seemed to get on so well. Megan was gorgeous, and so good with the children, wagging her short little tail at them and giving everyone friendly licks. She wasn't overwhelmed by all the excited hands reaching out to stroke her. She seemed to be taking it in her stride, and happily agreeing to be friends with everyone.

'I told the family what lovely pets Patterdales make and was delighted that they seemed to love Megan so much. They had been told she was tricky to handle off the lead, but now she was going to training classes, and they were happy to accompany her. They said they definitely wanted her and I was really pleased because they seemed like the perfect new owners for such a sweet little dog.'

But poor Megan! That home wasn't to be, either.

'A few days later, I was surprised to hear that the family had failed their "home visit". That's when a member of Dogs Trust staff visits the house to make sure it's suitable for the dog. They discovered that a rabbit was living in the house too, and since Megan may have been a rat-catcher in the past, Dogs Trust thought her living with a rabbit would be a recipe for disaster! The family quickly said they would get rid of the rabbit, but we felt that this was not a responsible attitude to have towards pets. What if they decided they wanted a cat in future? Would they be willing to get rid of Megan?'

Staff at Dogs Trust couldn't risk Megan being abandoned yet again, so they decided she would stay at the centre for a bit longer. Natalie felt sorry that Megan was having such a hard time finding a proper home, and allowed the little dog to sit in her office with her. It was fun for Megan, who loved human company, and Natalie found Megan a joy too.

'I quickly noticed how receptive she was,' says Natalie. 'I would be sitting at my desk planning a lesson, and all I had to do was glance at her and her tail would start wagging. I love all dogs, but there was something about Megan's character that really got me. She was just brilliant.

'I started to wonder if I could be the owner she was looking for. But if I was going to get another dog, I thought, it would have to be one I could take with me into schools. Ealy was getting older, and Belle could do with having another doggy colleague to share the workload. It takes a special sort of character to be an education dog, and I was sure Megan had it. Since I'd known her, she had shown a definite talent for being fussed over, while staying poised and patient and adorable. I would even love the challenge of training her how to behave properly when she was out on her walks.

'As I was thinking this through, I looked down to where Megan was relaxing with her chin on her front paws. I caught her eye, her tail gave a cheeky wag, and that was that. I took that wag as a yes. I went over and gave her a hug, and she was as delighted as always to be cuddled. I knew she'd be the best education dog ever.

'And sure enough, she is. She moved in with us in November and had a few weeks to settle in. Then, after Christmas, I introduced her to a group of schoolchildren that I knew would be gentle with her. Just as I thought, Megan took to teaching like a duck to water. She loves meeting and greeting lots of new people, so she's a great ambassador for Dogs Trust, and for dogs in general.

'When you watch Megan doing the job she loves, it's amazing to think of the journey she went through to get there. But as a reminder, I've got all the ticks that she had removed when she first arrived at Dogs Trust in a jam jar. When I'm teaching a lesson about dog grooming, I bring out the jar and rattle it. I ask the class where they think all those little blood-sucking creatures came from, and everyone's shocked when they learn they were once buried in the skin of the beautiful glossy dog at the front of the room. She's come a long way since those days!

'I involve Megan a lot in my lessons, and because she responds so well to people, she behaves like a proper little performer. She's patient and kind too, and the least scary dog I have ever known.

'Every morning I call out for one of my dogs to come to school, and it's almost always Megan who eagerly races to join me. And if there's a car journey – even better!'

Going to work is brilliant, as far as Megan's concerned, but at the end of a long day she's happy to come home again too. 'Megan and Belle are inseparable in the house,' Natalie says. 'If they've been away from each other all day, in the evening they leap around together covering each other in licks. They're adorable to watch.'

Megan's off-lead training is coming on well too. With lots of help from training and behaviour experts at Dogs Trust, she's learning the proper way to behave off the lead. Now, on her daily walks, she comes back when Natalie calls her.

'She really is improving,' says Natalie, 'but the temptation to go wild on a special woodland walk is still too much for her to resist. When I let her off the lead she still runs all over the place – after birds, squirrels and rabbits, into bushes and streams, out of all control but having a wonderful time.

'I take all sorts of treats with me to tempt her to come back when I call her. I've even taken a fresh, warm bacon sandwich, wondering if that might be the one thing that brings her back. But I haven't found that magic treat yet, and she still only comes back when she's tired and ready to go home. To be honest, I don't really mind. Megan is such a well-behaved professional when she's at work, she deserves to let her fur down in her time off!'

Arrow Finds a New Direction

Greetings, fellow dog-lovers.

Here at Dogs Trust we like to say it's *deed not breed* that makes dogs act the way they do. That means it doesn't matter what we dogs look like, it's how you treat us that counts. Just like people, a puppy who has been well brought up, who has been loved, cared for and understood, will grow up to be happy. And just like happy people, happy dogs are friendly, well-balanced and great to be around.

I know what you're thinking, and you're absolutely right, my upbringing has been particularly excellent. But for those who are less lucky than me, for those poor souls who have had a rougher start in life, and have maybe set off in a bad direction – all is not lost!

When you read Arrow's tale you'll see that anyone

can turn their life around, and a 'bad' dog turned good was maybe not that bad to start with ...

Lots of licks,

Poppy xxx

Arrow loves feet. 'It's true,' says his owner Wolfie. 'Licking feet is his favourite thing in the whole world. If someone comes into the room wearing sandals, he'll clean their feet for them. And at bedtime, the bottom of the quilt goes up and his little head pops in there searching for toes.'

Many people who don't know Arrow would find it hard to believe this stocky little English bull terrier/Staffordshire bull terrier cross would be so soppy. But then there's a lot about Arrow you wouldn't believe, especially if you knew what his past was like.

Tiny Arrow was brought to Dogs Trust Evesham with the rest of his litter when he was only six weeks old. Have you ever seen a litter of bull terrier puppies that small? They usually make an irresistible mound of wriggling velvetiness, full of uncontrollable joy and giving a hundred little licks a minute.

Arrow's litter was unfortunately not like that at all.

'They were a nightmare,' says the manager, Chris. 'We don't know what had happened to them before they came to the centre, but there was a lot of scrapping going on between them. One fight was so serious that it took two members of staff to break it up. So we had no choice but to separate the litter.'

The kennels were all full at the Evesham rehoming centre so little Arrow was moved to Dogs Trust Darlington. He had his neutering operation, and his own cosy kennel with lots of toys and blankets. Because of his unsettled early days, staff thought it would be simply too risky to give him a kennel-mate. So they wrote about Arrow's difficult start on his kennel sign, and hoped someone would want to rehome him soon so he could grow up in a loving home. It was sad that he hadn't experienced a normal family yet.

But Arrow did not enjoy life in kennels, and whenever people walked past him he would make a bad impression. He was rowdy. He would run around manically in his kennel, and didn't have a clue how to behave in company. He also took to chasing his tail round and round. Tail-chasing can be a sign of boredom and frustration in dogs.

Arrow was so stressed that one day he had a nasty accident. He bit his tail so hard he had to have part of it amputated by the vet. It was a very upsetting time for the poor dog, as well as for all the staff at the centre. They agreed that something needed to be done. The rehoming centres are lovely places and the staff do everything they can for the dogs, but often they just haven't got time to give the individual attention that some special residents need.

Arrow was so unhappy the staff decided he needed to get away from the hustle and bustle of the centre for a while. He should go back down to Dogs Trust Evesham, where there was a dedicated training centre. The training and behaviour advisers (TBAs) there would work with him to understand exactly why he was so unhappy. And with lots of individual care they would try and make him better.

Staff put a special profile on the Dogs Trust website for Arrow. They gave him a large kennel at the training centre, with a big raised bed and lots of comfy bedding.

And then they lavished him with what he really craved – attention.

'I must admit when I first met Arrow, I wondered what on earth we were going to do,' says Jane, a TBA at the training centre. 'He was so focused on chasing his tail he couldn't even hear what we were saying to him. He had fallen into his repetitive behaviour because he didn't know what to do with himself and it was a way of letting out his stress. When I looked at the poor lad, I wondered, with his behaviour, his history, and all the bad publicity about bull breeds at the time, would we ever find him a home?'

Jane quickly realised Arrow was a bright dog who had been in a boring environment, and that was what was leading him astray. 'We had to focus on keeping his mind occupied,' she says. 'We gave him lots of normal training, which he took to extremely well. He was a very keen dog – he loved being with people and getting involved in things. We always made sure he had chews and toys around to keep him busy when we weren't there, and we gave him lots and lots of exercise to make sure he slept properly.'

The TBAs at Dogs Trust are well trained in the best techniques for understanding doggy behaviour. They think understanding dogs is not so different from understanding people. 'For example,' Jane explains, 'if you're dying for the loo, you can't really pay attention to the person talking to you. If you haven't had enough sleep, you are more likely to snap at somebody who asks you a question. It's all the same with dogs.'

Arrow's behaviour really started to improve once he was at the training centre. 'It's amazing how quickly he came around,' says Jane. 'With a lot of dogs it's a long process even to *start* the process, but Arrow's behaviour began to improve early on. He was actually a lovely dog but he'd tear about without any self-control. He was so enthusiastic, but there was never any nastiness with him. He was just very, very lively.'

So, even though he had a long way to go, Arrow was coming on in leaps and bounds and growing happier all the time. And then one day, fate turned a corner in the young lad's life. Wolfie, a lady from Harwich, spotted him as she was browsing the Dogs Trust website. She couldn't stop looking at his picture and reading through his profile and so, one day, with her husband John, she travelled 185 miles from Harwich to Evesham to come and meet him.

Arrow was labelled a 'special needs dog' because of everything he had been through. 'We had to make it clear how important it was that his new owner would spend lots of time with him,' says Jane. 'If he didn't work on his training and keep his mind active, his boredom and frustration would come back. Again, like people, if a bright dog doesn't have enough to do, he will find bad ways of entertaining himself, and possibly even turn to mischief.'

Wolfie has a condition which means she uses a wheelchair. 'Arrow was called a special needs dog. Well I'm a special needs person, so we're the perfect match!' she says. 'My condition makes some basic things in life quite difficult, like picking up things I've dropped, opening doors and so on. So as well as a pet, I was half-looking for a dog I could train to help me with those things.

'I knew bull terrier assistance dogs were unheard of, but I didn't mind, because when I saw Arrow in the flesh, I simply thought *I want that dog!*'

Arrow bounded into the room at breakneck speed and hurled himself through the air on to John's lap. With no mean intentions but no manners either, the young chap had made his introduction. But Wolfie and John loved him instantly and they all really hit it off. By the end of the meeting, Arrow had even calmed down a bit.

'Arrow was a handful, but I could tell he had lots of focus in there somewhere,' says Wolfie. 'I knew we would have fun training together, and plenty of training was exactly what he needed. I didn't have a dog at the time but I've had six dogs before and for a long time I've been interested in training and understanding doggy behaviour. I decided it was time to start Project Arrow!'

Before Wolfie and John could take the boisterous bull terrier home, they had to make an appointment for someone from Dogs Trust to visit their house, to make sure it would be a nice home for a dog. Wolfie and John made the appointment, said goodbye to the excited Arrow, and drove the 185 miles back to Harwich. All the way they chatted about the crazy little dog and how they hoped they could rehome him.

The day of the home visit came. Nobody could believe how perfect Wolfie was for Arrow. From worrying that they would never find him a home, Arrow's carers at Dogs Trust now believed they had found him the best home possible. 'It was so lovely that there was someone who recognised how much Arrow had to offer,' says Jane. 'Wolfie saw through all the worries and behaviour problems to the lovely dog that we saw in him. We were certain Wolfie was the right handler, and so when her house passed the home visit, it was decided. Our Arrow had found his new home.'

Because the rehoming centre was so far away, Arrow had come along for the home visit too. Once the home was approved, the lady from Dogs Trust went back to the car. She opened the door and, although Arrow didn't know it at the time, when he leapt out, he was leaping into a whole new life.

'When he hurtled into the house, he definitely remembered us. He was jumping around all over us,' says Wolfie. 'But once the meet and greet was over, he calmed down. He was a bit restless and confused later that night because he didn't know why he hadn't gone back to his kennel. But we paid him lots of attention and played games with him, and once he was tired enough he settled down and went to sleep.'

A few days passed but, as everyone suspected, it wasn't long before Arrow's mischievous side came out. He took a particular interest in a quilt, and tore little holes in it with his teeth. 'He picked out hundreds of little balls of stuffing and stacked

them carefully in a heap,' laughs Wolfie. 'It looked like he was trying to build a snowman! It took us a while to get him to stop doing it, but it was so hilarious the first time we saw the snowman we couldn't stop laughing.'

Arrow also wasn't very well-behaved on his walks. 'He didn't have a clue how to act,' Wolfie says. 'As far as he was concerned, you greeted another dog by jumping on them. Of course, this didn't go down well with more polite dogs, who thought he was being aggressive and snapped back at him. He was actually only being friendly in a boisterous way, but it was a major problem we had to address.'

Wolfie and Arrow's first training session together was at a local dog training club called Scruffs. The class was held in one room with lots of other dogs, so Arrow even began to pick up some doggy manners. He enjoyed learning again, and his behaviour began to improve straight away.

But one day, this bull terrier bulldozer did something awful. John was throwing a ball for him in the garden, when the ball flew over the fence into the bushes next door. As John was chatting to the neighbour and they were trying to find the ball, the little boy from next door wandered into Arrow's garden. With his ball lost in the bushes, Arrow was delighted to have something else to play with, and with his characteristic rowdiness, he leapt on the child to say hello. Of course, the little boy was stunned and flew backwards on to the grass with the muscley dog on top of him. There was a bit of a scramble, and Arrow couldn't resist trying to take off the boy's shoes and socks to get inside and give his feet a lick.

'No one was hurt, but it was a big shock for the boy and I knew we couldn't go on like this,' says Wolfie. 'So, as well as his normal training, I started taking Arrow to see a special doggy behaviourist. We really began to see improvements after that.'

One day, a few weeks later, Wolfie had a big surprise. 'I dropped an orange on the floor,' she says. 'I couldn't reach it from my wheelchair so, without being asked, Arrow picked up the orange and very gently handed it back to me. I couldn't believe it − there were no teeth marks and no slobber. I was touched by what he had done for me. Straight away, I wondered if we could teach him a bit more.

'I started with his toys. I taught him the names

of his ball, his bone and his rag toy and lay them down in front of him. I then asked him to hand me whichever one I asked for. When he got it right, I gave him a treat.'

Arrow loved the game, and loved the treats that came with it. Garlic peanuts were his absolute favourite. 'These days, as soon as something hits the floor, he picks it up and hands it to me,' says Wolfie, proudly. 'And because I saw he enjoyed the praise that came with doing something useful, I wanted to teach him more.

'Arrow has always loved jumping up – that's part of what makes him the dog he is. I didn't want to get rid of that behaviour completely, but I didn't want him to jump on people. So I decided to teach him how to open and close doors. I tied a piece of rope to the door handle, and taught him the command *pull*, which means he should jump up, grab the rope and pull it down.'

The next lesson was *push*. Arrow would jump up and lean against the door with his solid little body. By teaching him *pull* and *push* instead of *open* and *close*, it did not matter if it was a door that opened inwards or one that opened outwards.

'He loved those lessons, because he got a treat every time he got it right,' laughs Wolfie. 'In fact, all the training has been a big game for Arrow since day one. He thoroughly enjoys it and I think that's the best way – learning is supposed to be fun!'

The next step was to teach Arrow how to find things. Wolfie would put his bone down in a different room, and then ask him to find it. 'He was getting the hang of that,' she says, 'so I wondered if we could take it a step further. I put my brush on the bed and then left the room and asked Arrow to find it. Off he went. I don't think he knew what he was supposed to be looking for but he found the thing that looked the most obvious, and he came back with it. Well, I praised him to high heaven for that.'

And now, Arrow knows the words for lots of different things. As well as picking up anything his owner drops, he can find her brush, book, pen and slippers. But that's not all he does!

'He can now even empty the washing machine,' chuckles Wolfie. 'Teaching him that was really funny because he hated putting his head in things. If I ever gave him a pot to lick out he would extend his tongue carefully into it, unlike most dogs, who would just shove their whole face in.

'So I used another favourite snack of his – onion ring crisps. I opened the door of the empty washing machine, placed an onion ring inside, and asked him to get it. He wasn't really comfortable with that idea, so I put another one closer to the edge. He got the one from the edge and I praised him. Then I encouraged him again to eat the one inside the machine. And, very reluctantly, he put his head in and whipped it out quickly with the crisp.

'We did that a few times to get him used to it and he soon realised that putting his head in the washing machine wasn't such a terrible thing.

Then I put a pair of trousers in the machine and an onion ring on top of them. He popped his head in and pulled out the crisp. After that I said "and the other one", which is a command I use when I want him to repeat an action. He pulled out the trousers and put them in the washing basket!'

Doing the laundry is now one of Arrow's favourite jobs, and he is also an expert at getting the post in the morning. 'Arrow especially loves getting the post because he gets three rewards for three jobs,' says Wolfie. 'If he does something particularly well in his behaviour, I give him one peanut, but for a proper job, he gets three. So he gets three garlic peanuts for opening the door, three for bringing me the letters and three for closing the door. He's still a bit naughty because he's worked out which letters are junk mail and he thinks it's fine to chew those ones up!'

So Arrow had learned some amazing things and, now that he had a proper job to focus his bright

Poppy the Dogs Trust Dog

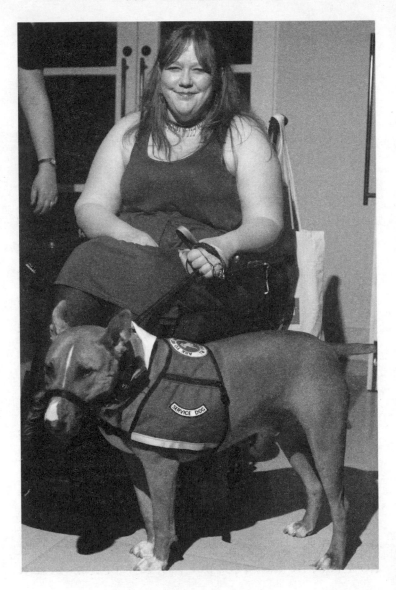

little mind on, his behaviour was much better too. In fact, when he was working, he was better behaved than you would expect from a normal dog! Wolfie decided she wanted to make him her official assistance dog. That would mean he could legally accompany her wherever she wanted or needed to go, like shops, offices and restaurants.

But making that happen proved very difficult indeed.

She found organisations in the UK wouldn't approve a dog they hadn't trained themselves, so she started looking overseas. 'I searched and searched and found an organisation in America who said they would be happy to approve Arrow, and being certified by them would count in the UK too. It wasn't cheap, but it needed doing and I was over the moon.

'The organisation asked for all sorts of information about him. He had to have a report from an official dog behaviourist saying he could do lots of different tasks: get out of a car and cross the road calmly, not push through doorways, be calm around children and other dogs, stay where he was asked to, and many other things. I am proud to say that Arrow can now do all of them perfectly.'

So Wolfie supplied the information the organisation asked for, signed a contract and two weeks later Arrow's special blue coat arrived. And now, as her official assistance dog, he is allowed to accompany her wherever she goes. 'Having Arrow with me all the time makes a huge difference to my life,' she says. 'I am so, so proud of him. And now, when we go out we get stopped all the time by admirers who want to meet him and ask me about him. We nipped to the supermarket the other day for a loaf of bread, and came out two hours later!'

Arrow has had his fair share of media attention too. You can see a video of him on *YouTube* and, as well as appearing in national and local newspapers, he featured in an impressive centre spread for *Bull Terriers Monthly*.

'When he's working, Arrow is totally calm and completely focused,' Wolfie says. 'But he still goes wild in his time off. Now that he knows the acceptable way to channel that wildness, it's not a problem at all. In fact I love him for it. He adores squeaky toys, although they don't last longer than five minutes, and I buy him huge rawhide chews as a thank you for all that he does for me.'

She has only owned Arrow for fifteen months, but friends who haven't seen him for a while are astounded by the change. Some even ask Wolfie if he's a different dog. 'I've been asked to give talks on how I turned Arrow into the dog he is today,' says Wolfie. 'So I'm sorting that out now. I'm looking forward to helping other people turn their dogs' lives around.'

Jane, the TBA at Dogs Trust Evesham, says, 'Wolfie has been a fantastic owner for Arrow. He is such a bright dog that he needed a job to do, and it's amazing how well he has done it. He hasn't just turned his own life around, he's also improved Wolfie's life. It just goes to show that absolutely anyone can be a valuable member of society with the right help.'

'Arrow is a great friend to me,' says Wolfie, 'and because I focus so much on what he's up to, I find I worry less about my own condition.'

When she's asked to describe Arrow in five words, Wolfie says, with a big smile and no hesitation, 'Best dog I've ever owned.'

Mr Magoo, Superstar

Well readers, what can I say?

I am so proud to have brought you this collection of stories. I hope you've enjoyed reading about some of the amazing dogs I've known, and the wonderful ways that Dogs Trust has helped them.

At Dogs Trust we know that, just like people, every dog is different, with their own special story to tell. And just like people, dogs sometimes need help to give their story a happy ending.

So, as a thank you to our four-legged friends everywhere for all the love, support, fun and happiness that they give to humans, Dogs Trust promises never to give up on a dog in its care. And all the money it takes to make that promise comes from donations from dog-lovers just like you. So thank you too!

Just think – so far you have only met nine of the sixteen thousand dogs that Dogs Trust helps every single year.

And your tenth story? Well ...!

Dear readers, it is my honour to introduce you to one of my very best friends – the one and only Mr Magoo!

Bye bye for now.

With all my love and licks,

Pops xxx

As soon as a new year begins at Dogs Trust Roden, and Louise the rehoming centre manager buys a new diary, the page of the twentieth of April begins to fill up with scrawled notes.

When spring arrives, the page is chock-a-block with scribbles, crossings-out and more scribbles. In the weeks leading up to the big day, the phone behind reception rings non-stop and all the staff are rushed off their feet.

And then, finally, the twentieth of April arrives …

'The staff enjoy Mr Magoo's birthday almost as

much as he does!' Louise says. 'There is such a buzz of excitement in the rehoming centre on that day. And even though he is centre of attention all year round, Gooey knows all the fuss he gets on his birthday is extra special. He loves it!'

The postman always grins as he comes up the path on the lucky lurcher's birthday, balancing a big stack of cards and parcels. And then all day long, the rehoming centre is busy with Mr Magoo's fans and sponsors who stop by with treats, toys, cards and cuddles.

'This year, Gooey started his birthday with a special breakfast of sardines and chicken, while we decorated his kennel with all the cards and pictures his fans had sent him,' says Louise. 'He wolfed down his breakfast, but when we opened the rehoming centre for the day, that's when the real fun began.

'He had lots of visitors this year. So many fans want to see him all year round that they have to book special appointments to spend some time with him. And on his birthday, Mr Magoo's visiting timetable is always packed!

'His guests take him out to the fields next to the rehoming centre where they can play and run about together. Mr Magoo's biggest fans know his favourite treats are Schmackos, so they bring some along for him as a birthday surprise.

'Some of our other dogs would be completely overwhelmed by all the attention, but Gooey adores it. Even so, we do make sure he gets some quiet time in his kennel during the day so he doesn't get too exhausted.

'Mr Magoo knows what his job is and he does it really well — like a wise old owl. He's been there and done it all before, and takes any task in his stride, with a wag of his tail and a big smile on his face.'

If you haven't heard of Mr Magoo before, you may be itching to know who he is and why on earth everyone makes such a fuss of him?

Well, Mr Magoo's story begins seven years ago

when, like many other Dogs Trust residents, a local dog warden brought him into the rehoming centre. The warden had found him wandering around the area by himself, with no collar, no owner and no home to go to.

Sometimes stray dogs are simply lost – their owners love them and desperately want them to come home. Dog wardens are always happy when they can reunite a lost dog with a worried owner, but unfortunately this doesn't always happen. And in other cases, a stray dog has been abandoned on purpose.

'Of course, a dog can't tell us what has happened in the past,' says Louise, 'so we can only guess by how he or she behaves. In Mr Magoo's case, I think his owner abandoned him. I have a feeling he didn't get much love and care in his old life, and I think it's likely he was told off a lot. He could have been bought as a puppy by someone irresponsible and then chucked out of his home when he became too big. We'll never know for sure.'

It's true that the lovely brown and white lurcher is big! With his slender body and long, powerful legs, Mr Magoo is also an amazingly fast runner. After he has been running he pulls the corners of his mouth back into a wide smile and his big brown eyes shine with happiness. Running is actually his second favourite thing, after cuddles, which he also can't get enough of.

'It's so sad to think that our Gooey may have been abandoned,' says Louise, 'because we think he's simply amazing, with the loveliest personality a dog could have. But whatever happened to him in his past has left him feeling insecure in some ways, and those worries have made it difficult to find the right home for him. We've tried really hard, but it hasn't ever quite worked out.

'Of course, when people see him happy in his kennel and what a friendly, affectionate chap he is, they often want to take him home. But over time we have discovered that he's quite an odd bod!

Gooey has tried a few homes – we checked each one out carefully and crossed our fingers that he would like it. But each time he got worried, confused and upset, no matter how lovely the home was, and how caring and patient the owner.

'He was always much happier here in his kennel at the rehoming centre. For example, he always had loads of doggy friends here and really liked sharing his kennel with a pal, but in the home he didn't like other dogs one bit.

'And he got upset and jealous if he was asked to share anything when he had his own home, even though here in the centre he was the kindest gentleman you could imagine.'

It was very puzzling because dogs, like people, usually love having their own home with lots of their own space and a close, caring family. One thing the staff at Dogs Trust Roden knew for certain was that Mr Magoo was a very special dog. So everyone worked hard for several years searching for Mr Magoo's perfect home – one where he could finally relax and keep being the happy, friendly dog they knew he really was.

One day, Louise was thinking about how important Mr Magoo was to the life of Dogs Trust Roden. 'I was thinking how Gooey loved being here and we loved having him here,' she says. 'He was happier here than anywhere else – and everyone enjoyed spending time with him too. All our volunteers were always delighted to walk Mr Magoo, because they got to watch his amazing running and then he liked lots of cuddles afterwards. He loved the company of people and it never seemed to bore him.

'Our lovely long-timer Mr Magoo was clearly really content and settled living at the rehoming centre, but he had so much more love and fun to give. I thought to myself – what better job could there be for a dog like Gooey than becoming a sponsor dog? Visitors would make a big fuss of him, which he would love, and he would be a marvellous ambassador for Dogs Trust.'

Being a sponsor dog is a very special position of responsibility for a Dogs Trust resident. Sponsor dogs are a way for dog-lovers to keep in touch with a real four-legged friend if they can't have one of their own. Even people who do have dogs sometimes like to sponsor one too, to help Dogs Trust look after them and all the other stray and abandoned dogs that the charity takes care of.

Sponsor dogs send their fans pictures,

certificates and updates about what they have been up to recently, so they get to become quite famous in the dog-loving community.

Most of the sponsor dogs are 'sticky dogs', who are looking for such special homes that they may be in the rehoming centre for a long time before they find the right one. So, some of them aren't keen on visitors because nasty experiences in their past have made them worried around people they don't know.

Mr Magoo is the opposite!

He has been a sponsor dog for two years, but he has now got more admirers than Louise ever thought was possible. 'He makes friends quicker than anyone else I know!' she laughs. 'Some of his fans travel for miles to come and see him and take him out for walks. They really can't get enough of the Mr Magoo magic!

'Just listen to this example of the sorts of fans he has. There is a lady who books her summer holiday really near to the rehoming centre every single year, just so she can come and walk Mr Magoo every day!'

And it is not just sponsors who love Dogs Trust Roden's leading lurcher. As an ambassador for his charity (and a very good sport), Mr Magoo does lots of visits of his own. He's out and about so often that he has become a real local celebrity.

It seems that as soon as people run their fingers through Mr Magoo's flossy brown and white fur and look into his wise eyes, they fall in love with him instantly.

'Sometimes teachers call the rehoming centre to ask if we can come and talk to the children about Dogs Trust,' says Louise. 'And what could make a lesson about dogs more exciting than having Mr Magoo in the classroom?'

The laid-back lurcher waits patiently at the front of the class, wagging his tail at all the admiring faces while someone from Dogs Trust talks about him and the other dogs at the centre. When the lesson is over, the children come up to greet him one at a time. And in an instant, Mr Magoo has made a whole room full of new two-legged friends.

He goes to lots of other special events and doggy days out throughout the year too. One of his favourite parts is travelling in the car. 'He always bounds in really eagerly,' says Louise. 'I think it's because he knows he is going to be doing something special when he gets out!

'Just recently we took Gooey along to a big walk-a-dog day, which had been set up to show that dogs are allowed on a special piece of local land. Well, this lovely place provided the perfect scenery for everyone to watch Mr Magoo run. Seeing our lightning-fast lad flash along the grass and through the trees made us feel very proud.'

Very few people experience the level of fame that Mr Magoo has achieved, but for him it's like water off a duck's back. 'He's so confident and noble,' says Louise. 'No attention is too much for Mr Magoo – he's a real showman.

If he were a human, he would probably be on the stage or in movies, acting in the most important leading roles!'

Because he is a dog, however, Dogs Trust Roden's open days provide the stage for Mr Magoo's biggest public performances. Open days are special days when lots of dog-lovers come to the rehoming centre to have a fun day out and show their support for all the work that Dogs Trust does for dogs in need.

Of course, the open days at Roden attract many of Mr Magoo's fans. People who sponsor him, or have met him at school, or have read about him in the newspaper, or have seen him at one of his many other public appearances come from miles to meet him.

The afternoon before the open day, everyone at the rehoming centre gets excited. Outside, volunteers set up lots of little stalls and tents and slowly fill a giant brightly-coloured bouncy castle with air. In the centre of the main field they peg a big show-ring into the grass.

Early the following morning, the area around the centre buzzes even more frantically as people fill up their stalls with toys and nick-nacks to sell, and games to play. Some stands are piled high with cakes and biscuits, and the sound of tinkling tunes fills the air as ice cream vans pull in to the fields. There are some stalls run by Dogs Trust staff who talk proudly about their work at the centre. Plenty of doggy toys are for sale, and some stands even sell home-made cakes especially for dogs.

The big tents also have lots of different and wonderful things inside them. One has face painting and a raffle, one has lots of bric-a-brac stalls, one sells refreshments … and one is Mr Magoo's very own tent!

At eleven o'clock on the morning of the big day, when everything is set up and ready, balloons are flying in the sky and doggy music is playing across the fields, Louise opens the rehoming centre gates. Crowds of excited people and dogs flood into the fields. The long-awaited open day has begun.

People and dogs greet each other excitedly and working dog displays in the show-ring amaze the audience. Little crowds gather around every stall, ice creams are slurped, and doggy cakes snuffled up by thrilled family pets.

And in the midst of all the action, Mr Magoo is doing just what he does best.

The legendary lurcher spends much of the day in his special tent, walking around greeting his crowds of adoring visitors with licks and wags. Lots of toys and goodies are for sale – all with Mr Magoo's famous face on them – and people queue up eagerly to have their picture taken with the great dog himself.

If people wander into the tent not knowing who Mr Magoo is, then his canine carer is there to tell them his story, and what he does in his important job as a sponsor dog. Needless to say, after meeting the affectionate dog and hearing his tale, whoever comes in to that tent always leaves it a big Mr Magoo fan.

He parades around the main field too, making new friends, both human and doggy. His groomed chestnut and white fur glistens in the sunlight as he slinks along, and his elegant neck sports a bright yellow Dogs Trust collar.

'Open days are the perfect opportunity for Mr Magoo to show off his charming character, and by the end of the day, you can be sure that his admirers have always doubled or tripled in number,' says Louise.

'He is so adored by everyone who meets him that we never give up hope that we will find Gooey that special, perfect home he so deserves. But we don't want to give him any more stress by trying new homes if we think he might not like them.

'He is so happy here at the centre – I really do think he has a whale of a time. He knows he's

Poppy the Dogs Trust Dog

pretty special and just loves all the attention that comes with being a star.'

As such a natural celebrity, it is no wonder that the lucky lurcher has collected huge boxes of letters and pictures from his fans over the years. 'We love reading all Mr Magoo's mail,' says Louise. 'Lots of the things that people send him get displayed on his kennel, and then we keep everything in his fan mail archive.'

So what does the future hold for Mr Magoo? 'Well where do I start?' says Louise. 'Next week, we're giving him a kennel makeover. We're planning to repaint all the walls and hang new pictures on them. He'll also be getting a beautiful, elegant, purple sofa that was donated to him by one of his fans. He loves lying on his sofa, and we think this gorgeous new one will suit our VIP dog Gooey down to the ground. Daffy Dove, his much-adored kennel-mate will enjoy lying on it with him too.

'Because he was so busy on his birthday, he

didn't have time for his usual birthday outing so we're also planning a special day for him. We'll take him to one of his favourite places – Barmouth Beach where he can run for miles along the sand, or Ellesmere Lake, where he loves to chase the ducks.

'And of course, best of all, he's got all his visitors to see. He's busy every weekend. And bank holidays, school holidays, Christmas, Easter, Valentine's Day – not to mention his birthday – are all enormous fun for Gooey.

'He's a real little star and definitely our most valued member of staff here at Dogs Trust Roden,' Louise says with a smile. 'Unless that one-in-a-million perfect home comes up, we wouldn't be without our Mr Magoo. And if ever we want to show off how laid-back, happy and affectionate our doggy residents can be, we know just whose kennel to head for.'

About Dogs Trust

Dogs Trust is the UK's largest dog welfare charity and we are working towards the day when all dogs can enjoy a happy life, free from the threat of unnecessary destruction.

We would like to solve the problem of so many unwanted dogs in the UK. We aim to do this by raising awareness about dogs, promoting dog welfare and encouraging responsible dog ownership.

We have seventeen Rehoming centres across the UK and help over 16,000 stray and abandoned dogs every year to find new, happy homes. We never put a healthy dog to sleep.

How to help

There are lots of ways you can support all our wonderful work for woofers in need. For example, many people like to help us through fundraising. Each year hundreds of people throughout the country take part in or organise events to raise money for our four-legged friends.

Find out more at www.dogstrust.org.uk/howtohelp/fundraiseforus

You can also sponsor a dog (like our lovely Mr Magoo) by visiting www.dogstrust.org.uk/sponsor_a_dog

If you would like to make a donation to Dogs Trust, you can do this at www.dogstrust.org.uk/howtohelp/donations

Dog-loving shopaholics can buy all sorts of doggy delights and support Dogs Trust at the same time. Just visit www.dogstrust.org.uk/howtohelp/shopping

Contact information

All the information you need about Dogs Trust can be found at www.dogstrust.org.uk, and there is also a special website for children and teachers at www.learnwithdogs.co.uk.

You can contact Dogs Trust's Head Office by writing to:

Dogs Trust
17 Wakley Street
London
EC1V 7RQ

Or telephone: 020 7837 0006

To find your local Dogs Trust rehoming centre, visit www.dogstrust.org.uk/rehoming/our_centres

Or if you already know where your local rehoming centre is and would like to help out, you can contact them on the telephone numbers over the page:

Ballymena	028 2565 2977
Bridgend	01656 725219
Canterbury	01227 792505
Darlington	01325 333114
Evesham	01386 830613
Glasgow	0141 773 5130
Ilfracombe	01271 812709
Kenilworth	01926 484398
Leeds	0113 281 4920
London (Harefield)	01895 453 930
Merseyside	0151 480 0660
Newbury	01488 658391
Roden	01952 770225
Salisbury	01980 629634
Shoreham	01273 452576
Snetterton	01953 498377
West Calder	01506 873459

Photo credits

Cover

Front cover photo © Pat Doyle

Back cover:

Top and bottom photos © Andy Catterall

Middle photo © Stanford Photographic

Foreword: pix © Andy Catterall

Poppy: p5, p7, p10, p19 © Pat Doyle

Cracker: p53, p60 © Stanford Photographic

Weasel: p77, p95, p96 © Media Wales

Jess: p127, p141 © Nick Ridley Photography

Oakfield Oldies: p151, p163, p166 © Andy Catterall

Mr Magoo: p219, p226, p234 © Andy Catterall

*Poppy the Dogs Trust office dog shares more
heart warming stories of life at Dogs Trust in*

POPPY'S PUPPIES

From snowy the deaf pup who had to learn sign
language, to celebrities like Barney the Blue
Peter dog, these unforgettable tales show us the
range of Dogs Trust's work in rescuing dogs in
need.

And don't miss Poppy's Pointers – all you need
to know about becoming a puppy owner.